THE COMPLETE GUIDE TO BLOODHOUNDS

Kevin Stueber

LP Media Inc. Publishing

Text copyright © 2019 by LP Media Inc.

www.lpmedia.org

Publication Data

Kevin Stueber

The Complete Guide to Bloodhounds ---- First edition.

Summary: "Successfully raising a Bloodhound dog from puppy to old age" --- Provided by publisher.

ISBN: 978-1-09498-833-7

[1. Bloodhounds --- Non-Fiction] I. Title.

Design by Sorin Rădulescu

First paperback edition, 2019

TABLE OF CONTENTS

INTRODUCTION

Bloodhounds. Loving, intelligent, and strong creatures bred to have an exceptional sense of smell. They are majestic animals. They are large in stature and loyal to their owners. Bloodhounds love to work and love to please. But, even with all of their redeeming qualities, they do require a special owner who has what it takes to bring out the best in their dog. Bloodhounds are stubborn. They have one of the best noses in the dog world and they follow it above all else. When a Bloodhound locks onto a scent, they want to find it. Their appearance, with all their folds and wrinkles and long ears, is designed to make Bloodhounds master trackers.

And while those folds and flaps are excellent for catching a scent and sending it to the dog's powerful nose, they are also great for catching something else: drool. Out of all the dogs I've ever owned, none of them have ever slobbered, salivated, and spit as much as a Bloodhound. When the dog shakes its head, you better take cover. Slobber and spit will go flying in all directions. If you have any important artwork hanging on the walls, it's best to make sure they are behind glass. I learned that one the hard way.

If you're already reading this, you must be at least thinking about joining the elite group of Bloodhound owners. They are truly a joy to be around. They have strong personalities and make life anything but dull. But they do have some characteristics that I wish I had known about before getting one. None of those characteristics would have changed my mind about becoming a Bloodhound owner, but maybe having the knowledge I'm going to share with you would have prepared me for the journey I embarked on. So sit back, grab a towel, and get ready for a wild, and sometimes wet, ride.

CHAPTER 1
Bloodhounds – A History and Description of the Breed

Bloodhounds are an iconic breed of dog. They're used frequently in movies and TV shows depicting them as master trackers. One of the most common depictions of the dog is as one who can track down escaped convicts or prisoners. Country singer Blake Shelton even told a story about a Bloodhound named Ol' Red in one of his songs. In that story, no convict has ever been able to escape from the prison during the time the Bloodhound was on duty. Every time they try, the dog would sniff them out and track them down. But in the end, Shelton tells a story of making the dog fall in love with a different type of hound so that when the prisoner escapes, the Bloodhound tracks down his love, rather than the escaped prisoner. While the story in Shelton's song is romanticized a bit, the main subject is completely accurate.

Photo Courtesy of
Shyla Bryant

Introductory Facts About Bloodhounds

Bloodhounds have one of, if not the best, noses in the dog world. Their sense of smell is 40 times stronger than that of humans. Because of that sense of smell, the Bloodhound has been used by law enforcement and search and rescue teams to track people and things for a long time. In fact, the Bloodhound's ability and reliability to track is so good that it was the first animal whose evidence was admissible in court in the United States. Their nose is so reliable and strong that there are countless stories about the dogs following scents that are days or weeks old for miles at a time. The first time you see a Bloodhound, nose down, ears dragging alongside its head with its tail pointing at the sky, you'll truly understand why this dog is a marvel of the animal kingdom.

*Photo Courtesy of
Kendall Alguire*

Bloodhound Emergence and History

Part of the reason Bloodhounds are so good at tracking is because they have been doing it for at least a thousand years. Reports of Bloodhounds began emerging around 1000 A.D., when monks started recording their use. The dogs were supposedly bred and kept in an abbey in Belgium dedicated to St. Hubert. Because of that location, the dog was named the Hound of St Hubert. Even then, they were revered for their tracking abilities

Photo Courtesy of Erika Goforth

and were used primarily as hunting dogs. The only problem with them was that they got so big they were outperformed by other hounds. The Bloodhound was just too slow and for whatever reason, lacked the kill instinct needed to finish off the job in deer hunts.

As time went on, the Bloodhound's popularity dwindled. They were still used across Europe for hunting, but were replaced by dogs that could track and kill the animal they were following. In the twentieth century, the world wars in Europe affected life for everyone, including Bloodhounds. Bloodhound population shrunk and one of the main factors that led to their survival was their use by the United States in the prison system. Widespread use gave way to specialization and Bloodhounds were bred to fulfill the niche of tracking down missing persons in search and rescue situations. Owners in Europe still use them for fox hunts to this day, where large groups of hounds come together and track down a fox for sport. Their owners follow the sounds of the pack's barks, or "baying" as it's called, to find the animal in a show of gallantry and high society. But, whether Bloodhounds were tracking animals or people, their nose has been the one undeniable trait that has proved their usefulness for centuries.

Appearance and Color Variations

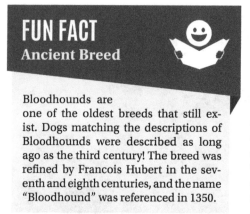

FUN FACT
Ancient Breed

Bloodhounds are one of the oldest breeds that still exist. Dogs matching the descriptions of Bloodhounds were described as long ago as the third century! The breed was refined by Francois Hubert in the seventh and eighth centuries, and the name "Bloodhound" was referenced in 1350.

Everything about a Bloodhound is designed to complement their nose. They are large dogs, easily weighing in at over 100 lbs. They grow fast and eat A LOT. The most iconic things people notice about Bloodhounds are their wrinkles, folds, and excess skin. They have long ears and so much excess skin on their face that they give their eyes a droopy appearance due to the weight of the skin pulling down on the lids under their eyes.

While many say this makes Bloodhounds look sad or pouty, all that excess skin actually serves a function. Their ears, big droopy jowls, and large lips all work in conjunction to direct scents and smells into the dog's nose. When a Bloodhound's head is down and their nose is to the ground, the excess skin collects the scent particles and funnels them to where they need to go. Their ears drag along the ground and actually block off sounds from distracting the dog while it focuses on its primary objective: the scent. Beyond its face, the Bloodhound is streamlined and sleek when young. Even their tail is long and pointed and will stand almost straight up when the dog is locked onto a scent. They are a prime example of how natural selection and selective breeding can influence a dog's looks and physical characteristics to achieve a goal.

Bloodhounds are relatively short-haired dogs and come in three primary color patterns. The most common Bloodhound is Black and Tan, where the dog is primarily black, with patches of brown in certain areas. The dog will usually have brown marks above their eyes, on their chest, and down their legs, while the rest of them is mostly black. It almost appears as if the dog is wearing a black saddle with a hood on it. Some variations will have more black, while others will have less. Another common coloration is Liver and Tan. This is similar to the Black and Tan, but rather than a black saddle, the dog has a reddish-brown primary coat color. The legs and accents are still brown. The last variation in color is the Liver Bloodhound. This is also referred to as a Red Bloodhound because they lack the contrasting colors of the previous two and exhibit just one all-over coat color. These are also referred to in some groups as "Georgia" Bloodhounds, presumably due to their prevalence in the Southern United States. Other dogs with similar appearances exist in the world, but true Bloodhounds will display one of the patterns and colorations listed above. This limited color scheme and definitive patterning helps lend the Bloodhound their unmistakable and iconic appearance.

Overview of Temperament and Behavior

"Bloodhounds are big ole teddy bears, their size can intimidate some people but they are gentle giants."

Kevin Weitkamp
Black River Bloodhounds

Now that we know what a Bloodhound looks like, it's time to answer the big questions: How does a Bloodhound act? Are they good with kids? What is their temperament like? While some of these items will be addressed in later chapters, there are some things to know early on to help in the decision of getting a Bloodhound. They are loyal and loving animals. It is not uncommon for them to lie around, keeping their favorite place on the porch warm. But that most likely won't come until they are a few years old. As puppies and up through their first couple of years, Bloodhounds have tons of energy. They love to play, run, bark, jump, and dig. They are surprisingly agile and many users report "counter surfing," where the dogs will somehow get themselves on top of countertops, tables, or anything high.

Photo Courtesy of
Diane Stradling

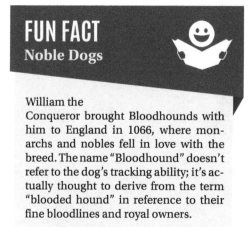

FUN FACT

Noble Dogs

William the Conqueror brought Bloodhounds with him to England in 1066, where monarchs and nobles fell in love with the breed. The name "Bloodhound" doesn't refer to the dog's tracking ability; it's actually thought to derive from the term "blooded hound" in reference to their fine bloodlines and royal owners.

Bloodhounds are good with kids and small animals with proper training, but their enormous size can be a problem. Because these dogs are so loving and believe to their core that they were meant to be lap dogs, they will sometimes forget how big they are and throw their weight around. It's important to keep an eye on small children and animals to make sure they aren't accidentally knocked over or stepped on. Bloodhounds love to love, but their size can sometimes work against them.

As discussed above, Bloodhounds are bred to follow a scent above all else. That means they will tune the rest of the world out when they lock onto something. They are dedicated and persistent in accomplishing what they set out to do. What that means to the owner is that Bloodhounds are stubborn. They don't always listen and can be tough to train. They are sensitive souls, and many times won't react to punishment so need lots of reinforcement and conditioning to get them to behave the way you want them to behave. Their persistence in tracking makes it extremely hard to allow them to be off their leash. The problem is that if they catch a scent they want to investigate, they will go for it and many times will disregard owner commands.

Along with stubbornness, Bloodhounds are vocal. They bark, or "bay" at anything that they want to draw attention to. Baying is the characteristic guttural, long howls that Bloodhounds let out. It almost sounds like the hound is yelling at whatever it is that is bothering them, and they get bothered by a lot of stuff. Bloodhounds are really big scaredy-cats and hate when things are out of place. It is not uncommon for them to see something new introduced into their environment and let you know about it by barking and baying at it. In all, Bloodhounds are great family dogs, but need someone willing to deal with their stubbornness and give them the attention they need to ensure they remain as gentle giants and not as big, lumbering nuisances.

Things to Consider Before Bringing a Bloodhound Into Your Life

Now that you have an idea of what a Bloodhound is and where they come from, it's time to ask yourself if having a Bloodhound is right for you. As evidenced by the above, they are great family dogs that can also be great working dogs. They are iconic in appearance and have a long history. But due to their size and energy when young, they do require space to run and grow. They are not dogs to keep in an apartment or locked up in a small room. They need room to run and play and need a patient owner who understands that the dog just wants to love their owner and do their job, but can sometimes have problems listening. They love the outdoors and thrive in wide open spaces, but follow their nose a bit much to be trusted on their own. They require attention and training to become the truly amazing dog they are destined to be. If you have what it takes to join the elite club of Bloodhound Owners, then congratulations. Life will never be the same after owning a Bloodhound. Your patience will be tried, but your heart will grow as you learn to love and live with this regal breed.

CHAPTER 2
Special Considerations and Special Needs

So now that you know the background of the breed, it's time for some insider information. The following are some things that I found out after getting my first Bloodhound. When I started research-ing dog breeds, I wasn't necessarily paying attention to things like intel-ligence or how much they shed, but was basing my decision solely on looks. I wanted a dog that stood out. Something different that people don't see every day. I wanted to be different. With that being my goal, I set to work searching through Google images and compiled a list of breeds I would want to bring home. As soon as I saw a Bloodhound, I stopped. I had only ever seen one in person, and he was a therapy dog that was just lying around at an event I had taken my family to.

So, based on that knowledge and minimal research, I set out to find a breeder and get a dog. Upon meeting the breeder, I got my first taste of the adventure I was about to go on. When I asked the breeder if there was anything special I needed to get for the puppy, she said, "You better get two mops. One for the floor and one for the walls." To this day, that advice has been the most honest thing I've ever been told about Bloodhounds.

The Drool Factor – Are You and Your Guests Ready for a Bloodhound

Bloodhounds are majestic. They stand out and they are great pets. We've established that part. But if there were a brochure that came with a Bloodhound, the fine print would forewarn of the gallons of endless slobber that a Bloodhound can produce. At times it seems like more liquid comes out of their mouth than ever goes in. They drool when they are happy. They drool

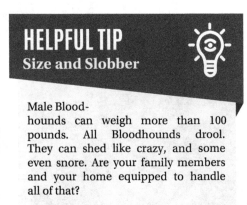

HELPFUL TIP
Size and Slobber

Male Bloodhounds can weigh more than 100 pounds. All Bloodhounds drool. They can shed like crazy, and some even snore. Are your family members and your home equipped to handle all of that?

when they are excited. They drool when they are scared. They drool. All. The. Time. The aforementioned folds of skin on their face and jowls are perfect receptacles to collect the copious amounts of slobber. And when those folds and flaps are filled to the brim, they overflow and drip without discrimination. And if the dog feels like shaking its head, the reserved drool turns into deadly slobber bombs on a collision course with anything that finds itself unlucky enough to be in its path. Drool will go flying in all directions and leave its mark on walls, appliances, clothes, bare skin, and any number of other things. When I got mine, the breeder wasn't lying. I now have a mop I use to get to the drool left by my Bloodhound on the out of reach spots on my wall.

I tell you this not to scare you, but rather to prepare a new owner for the very real expectations of having a Bloodhound. Having one requires extra cleaning to keep the home tidy. Neat freaks may have a slight panic attack if they choose to get a Bloodhound because cleaning up after them could easily be a full-time job. Having guests over can be equally tough as an excited dog can get extra frothy and drooly, and as they sniff and smell the newcomer, they may leave trails of saliva on clothing. It can be a turn-off for some people who really enjoy having a pristine home. Bloodhounds can't control when or where they drool, and if having a spotless house is important to you, you may be better off with a different breed. For me, I hang an apron by my front door so guests can cover up their clothing and leave without feeling like they need to take a shower and do a load of laundry. So Bloodhounds drool a lot. Some may see it as a downfall of the breed, but as long as you invest in a couple mops and an apron, you will be able to enjoy the companionship they have to give.

Size and Energy Cons

Photo Courtesy of Jessica Baldwin

Another thing to keep in mind about Bloodhounds is their size and what they can do with it. I've already mentioned that Bloodhounds can be lazy and are great family pets and while that's true, they can also be hardheaded balls of raw energy. Someone once summed it up perfectly by saying that for the first couple years, a Bloodhound pup will be one of the wildest puppies you've ever seen, but as they get to about three years old, their energy starts to decrease exponentially. This is important so you don't fool yourself like I did. Just because it's a Bloodhound puppy, doesn't mean it's not going to act like any other puppy. Be ready for the usual puppy behaviors. And be ready for a lot of those behaviors to lessen but continue into adulthood.

Energy – And Lots of it

As an adult, a Bloodhound will need plenty of room to run. If they are confined for too long or have excess energy to burn, they may resort to negative behaviors like digging or chewing to get that energy out. Being as powerful as they are, Bloodhounds can and will dig holes in a beautiful yard if they are bored. The key to preventing this is plenty of exercise and routine walks. Deborah S. Thompson from Cyclone Ridge Kennels sums it up perfectly by saying, "They will get bored easily if not matched correctly to your lifestyle and will dig to China either outside or in your new sofa." Although walking a Bloodhound has challenges all its own which we will cover later, it is a critical item to learn and work into your routine if you want to keep those destructive behaviors at bay.

Grooming and Shedding

With all the energy that Bloodhounds have, you can expect them to want to be outside quite a bit. And with all those low-hanging flaps of skin and dragging ears, Bloodhounds have the propensity to get dirty. It's not uncommon to find mud caked onto their ears that just dragged across the yard or dirt lodged up into their nostrils from their latest game

HELPFUL TIP

More Than Just a Bark

While most dogs bark, Bloodhounds have additional vocalizations including baying, howling, and whining. This may not be the best dog for you if you prefer to have a quiet home and pet.

of "What's That Smell?" These factors, coupled with the drool factor listed above, mean that Bloodhounds do require a bit of normal grooming and care to keep them, and you, clean. Regular baths are important and since dirt has the potential to hide in all the nooks and crannies on their face, an owner must take care to clean out lips, ears, and other crevices to ensure they are free from dirt and moisture. A buildup of either can lead to problems and yeast infections. Their ears have a particular tendency to become infected or bothersome, but regular care and baths can help combat most common afflictions. For those wondering how to keep a hundred-pound ball of energy in the bathtub I have two words: peanut butter. Put a dollop of the treat on the wall and that should occupy your hound long enough to wash them up without too many issues.

During bath time, it is not uncommon for Bloodhounds to shed quite a bit of their fur and clog up the drain. One may not think a Bloodhound would shed that much based on their short coat, but they do in fact shed quite a bit. This is due to their multiple coats. They have very fine, short hair, but they also have an undercoat which will shed with the seasons. The undercoat helps protect the dog from moisture and temperature fluctuations. As they are historically hunting dogs, they need to be in prime condition to be in the woods and able to survive the harshness of the wild. Even with the short coat, a lot of Bloodhounds love playing in the snow and their undercoat helps keep them warm. There are multiple factors which can help reduce shedding, including diet and maintenance. I feed my hound a diet that consists of Omega 3 fatty acids and an occasional raw egg. Both of these foods will help encourage the growth of a healthy, smooth, and shiny coat, but will not eliminate shedding altogether. Regular brushing and baths will also help minimize the fur balls you find around the house, but again, shedding is just part of the territory when owning a Bloodhound.

Stubbornness and the Need for a Confident Owner

The last special consideration a new owner should contemplate when getting a Bloodhound is probably the most important, and it revolves around their temperament. Bloodhounds are stubborn. There are no ifs, ands, or buts about it. The breed is notoriously hardheaded. Part of this comes from how they behave when following a scent and how they can tune the world out to focus on that one thing. But beyond when just out on walks, Bloodhounds are stubborn in all they do. They can be hard to train and seem like slow learners. They can act defiantly and resort to bad behaviors you thought you had trained away months or years before.

This, for me, is the hardest part of owning a hound. I have trained other dogs and been able to use punishment and reward to train behaviors that I expect of my pets, but with a Bloodhound, nothing seemed to work. It was frustrating and what initially led me to finding out so much about the breed. By learning of their intended purpose and their overall demeanor, I was able to gain some insight in how I had to change myself to be able to get my dog in control.

Training a Bloodhound can try your patience and make you question your decision to ever get one in the first place. For me, housetraining was one of the hardest obstacles I had to overcome. Walking out in the morning to wet carpets and buying cases of carpet cleaner to get rid of the smell was commonplace. No matter what I did, nothing, beyond locking my hound up in his crate at night, would stop the accidents. This led to frustration and desperation.

Photo Courtesy of Claire Bishop

My salvation was finally learning that it was me who had to change how I was handling the dog. I had to develop confidence and had to develop a routine. Getting angry and punishing the pup did nothing, as his stubbornness would just lead him to forget and do the behavior again the next day. It's important to know that a Bloodhound needs a leader. They need a

*Photo Courtesy of
Terri Senecal*

strong and confident person who will guide them in what they need to do and understands that only through reinforcement will the dog learn. By forming a routine, maintaining my composure, and showing the dog who was boss, I was finally able to make some headway. Bloodhounds believe that because of their size, they rule the roost by default. And, if an owner lacks confidence and a strong will that can match that of the dog, the dog will use its weight to do what it wants. But if an owner can find their inner alpha and learn to lead their dog, the Bloodhound will learn their place. While they may still push the boundaries from time to time, by exerting dominance and showing confidence, the owner can keep their dog in control and make living with a Bloodhound absolutely enjoyable. At least, that's what I try to tell myself.

CHAPTER 3
Making Sure Your Home Is Suitable for a Bloodhound

"Bloodhounds are not the lazy dog that lays a porch like most people think. These dogs are very smart and active. Having a bloodhound can be compared to having a 100 lb toddler. If they get bored, they will find something to get into."

Heather Pearson
Black Diamond Bloodhounds & Bracco Italianos

Existing Family and Pet Considerations

Having a Bloodhound is a decision that should be made only after taking all things into account. This means finding out if a Bloodhound will fit into your and your family's life and home. The shedding may cause allergy concerns. Their size may cause you to consider the size of your home and backyard. The age of children in the home and other existing pets must be considered to determine if a Bloodhound is the best fit for you and your family. While on the surface there are no glaring reasons why a Bloodhound can't fit into someone's life, individual experiences and circumstances can be the breaking point between getting one and finding a different breed.

Some Bloodhounds can show aggression around food or toys and some can have a chase instinct that makes them impulsively chase small animals and other pets. A dog's past can also play a role in how they behave and what triggers they may have depending on how old they are when you get them and what their previous environment was like. No two dogs are the same, and while breed does play a role in predicting behavior, environment and past experience will also influence how a particular animal behaves in the home.

One of the many things to think about is again the size of the Bloodhound. They are a big breed. Since they love to be close to their owners and cuddle, the potential exists for them to harm or hurt someone

Photo Courtesy of
Elaine Bartels

based on sheer weight alone. It's almost as if the dog doesn't understand their own strength. If they jump up on someone, they can easily knock them down. Since they are so large, most Bloodhounds could easily be taller than most children and some adults. Mine can look me in the eye when he stands on his hind legs and I'm six feet tall. When playing, they can throw their weight around and if they knock into someone, that person could take an unexpected fall.

These aren't reasons to avoid getting a Bloodhound, but rather considerations to take and to prepare for. Good training and creating ideal behaviors in your pet can make most of this avoidable. Of course there will still be accidents and a kid could get knocked over, but the breed isn't inherently violent or aggressive. I am preparing for a new baby and am fully aware of the work and attention that will go into keeping baby and dog safe. There will be training on all sides that needs to go into ensuring the Bloodhound is as gentle as possible with the baby. As the baby gets older, he will have to learn to respect the dog and his space. It's not that Bloodhounds can't be in a household with kids, but it requires extra training to make sure the kids and the dog respect each other and know each other's boundaries.

Protecting Your Furniture

Not only should someone consider the people and pets in their home prior to getting a Bloodhound, but they should also consider how much they like their furniture. Inevitably, having a puppy will lead to items being chewed on that may not be ideal. This could include loose articles of clothing, toys, and furniture. Some of this can be avoided by just making sure items you don't want chewed up are kept out of the dog's reach, but that's not always possible. The best way to stop a Bloodhound from chewing or destroying your furniture is to distract them with things that they CAN chew. Make sure your dog has plenty of toys of different styles. If the dog is content with the items you give them and those items work them out mentally and physically, they are less likely to engage in destructive behaviors.

Of course, training is a big part of this, as well as being attentive to your dog and not leaving them unattended in a room where they can get in trouble. Once the dog knows the boundaries and which toys are theirs, they will be less likely to destroy your things. Bloodhounds will also resort to destructive behaviors when bored and if experiencing anxiety. Toys will help combat boredom, and creating safe spaces for your dog within your home can help alleviate some of the anxiety they may experience when you are away or step out of the room.

Potential Risks for Other Pets and Small Children

Bloodhounds are instinctively territorial and protective of their families and the spaces they call home. It's not unheard of for Bloodhounds to be skittish around strangers and turn into guard dogs when someone new enters the home. This territorial aspect can expose some behaviors that may seem troubling at first, but with good training can be avoided.

As already stated, kids and Bloodhounds can bump heads because of the dogs' boisterous and aloof behavior. Kids can also add to this by wanting to get close to the dog while the dog is eating. Training a dog to not be aggressive around food is a battle with any breed, but can be especially difficult with a stubborn breed like a Bloodhound. The easiest way to avoid this is by establishing and reinforcing the dog's place in the pack. A dog must know that the child or pet is higher in rank than them. I trained my dog from a young age by feeding him one piece of food at a time from my hand. This showed the dog that I control the food and that I am in charge of when they eat. This instinctively led him to understand I had a better rank in the pack than him and that I was boss. This can be done with kids too as they can feed the dog, under adult supervision, until the dog begins to understand their place in the pack.

HELPFUL TIP
Small Children and Other Pets

While Bloodhounds usually love children and get along well with other pets, their sheer size and energy can make these relationships complicated. One whack of their tail could send a toddler tumbling, and a cat may be annoyed by the drool. Be sure to factor these things into deciding if a Bloodhound would fit into your family.

This can also be done with small animals. Holding a small animal while making the Bloodhound sit and watch you give attention to the other animal can teach that the other is a higher rank than they are and as such shouldn't be harassed or harmed. Obviously, these techniques require much more than what is outlined here, but provide a basic understanding of some of the work that must be done to prepare your Bloodhound to be around your other pets and small children.

Photo Courtesy of
Robyn Griffin-Mixan

Safe Spaces for Your Bloodhound

Along with the above ways of getting your Bloodhound to fit into your home, another crucial aspect of Bloodhound ownership is creating a safe space for your dog. Creating a safe space includes not only eliminating potential dangers to your dog's health, but also creating a safe and welcoming environment that your dog can call their own. It's important to inventory your house and try to get rid of or limit your dog's contact with potentially deadly house plants, household cleaners and poisons, and food. Many different plants can be toxic to dogs and if they are at a level the dog can

Photo Courtesy of Amanda Riddles

reach, they will most likely try to take a bite of it. That leaves the option of either moving the plant, or limiting the dog's access to the area in which it is housed. Certain human foods can also be deadly to dogs, so limiting their access to areas where food can be dropped may be the best option for keeping your pet safe. I tend to keep the dog out of the kitchen and ensure that any chocolate or candy is put away in a cabinet rather than being left out on the counter. Limiting access to areas where there are potential risks to your dog is the best way to avoid any health problems arising from them ingesting something they shouldn't.

Beyond limiting access to places in your home that pose potential risks, giving your Bloodhound a place of their own is important. Some people swear by crate training, which is getting a large cage or crate for your dog and making that their den. I was initially against this technique as I wanted my dog to be able to roam freely around my house. And although we eventually got to that point and he is no longer confined to his crate at certain times, he now chooses to go to his crate because it is his safe place. Getting a crate or doghouse which provides enough room for the dog to fully stand up and turn around in can be a great way to create a place for your Bloodhound to go and call their own. Crate training has other benefits with housetraining and potty training as well, but its role as a place for your dog to call their own is equally important. This will help them when you are away and they experience separation anx-

Photo Courtesy of
Tad and Jennifer Person

iety by providing security and, in turn, will limit some of the destructive behaviors that come about due to anxiety.

There are other ways of creating a space for your dog as well. Some people will get a dog bed or pillow of some sort and put it somewhere in the home and make that the dog's area. The dog can then go there and know it won't be bothered and use it as a way to communicate its needs back to you. Having a safe place in your home for your dog is good way to allow your dog and you to get some down time and to allow them to feel comfortable and happy.

Outdoor Spaces – Exercising the Brain and Body

Having an outdoor space for your hound is also necessary for creating an enriching environment. For some with lots of land, giving the dog a lot of room to run is a nice convenience, but should be paired with some sort of barrier to ensure the dog doesn't run off after something it smells. Other people may not have as much room for their hound to roam free and may have to utilize the space in their backyard. This can come with its own set of troubles, as making sure your landscaping is left intact can be a challenge.

Finding a place for your dog to relieve themselves without killing grass or plants is a challenge in itself which we will talk about later, but is something to consider when planning out your Bloodhound's territory. Getting them to go in a specific place isn't too difficult and there are aids which can help show them the right spot to do it.

Using landscaping fences and barriers is also a great way to keep dogs out of your garden. I planted some potatoes once, and within a few minutes, my hound had sniffed them out, dug them up, and had them on prominent display in the middle of the yard. By spending time outside with him and paying attention to his cues, I was able to train him on which places were okay to explore, and which areas were off limits. Conditioning and consistency are keys in teaching the dog where they are allowed to be. And, since Bloodhounds can be easily scared by seemingly mundane items, using those to your advantage can also help create a space that you and your hound can share. For me, the dog was scared of rakes. Leaning a rake against the wall by my garden was enough of a deterrent to keep the dog out. Once we established where my area was and where his was, I didn't have to worry about coming out to a pile of dirt and dug up potatoes.

CHAPTER 4
Choosing the Perfect Bloodhound for Your Lifestyle

"Most importantly, visit the facility and meet the dog or parents of a pup. Getting a Bloodhound with the right temperament is most important for a good match. If a good match is not made, neither the owner nor the pup/dog will be happy."

Nancy Boerner
Boerner's Bloodhounds

Photo Courtesy of April Conklin

Determining What You Want Your Bloodhound to Do (Tracking, Hunting, or Chilling)

"An experienced breeder should be able to evaluate pups to see which are best suited for families as a pet/companion and those best suited for working. A pup that is best fitted for a family home can usually be turned into a working hound, but it is almost impossible to take a pup deemed best for working and put into a typical family home as a companion pet."

Nancy Boerner
Boerner's Bloodhounds

Now that you've mentally prepared yourself for the trials and tribulations that are to come when raising a Bloodhound, it's time to figure out where you are going to get your pet. There are many options out there and choosing the one that best fits your expectations is important. There are many rescues that specialize in hounds and many breeders as well. Doing your research and finding a sensible and responsible place or person to get your dog is just as important as which dog you choose.

The first thing you'll have to consider is at what age you want to get your dog. A lot of people are going to want a puppy, and there are a lot of benefits to getting a dog so young. One of the main benefits, beyond how darn adorable puppies are, is that you will be able to control the environment the pup grows up in and start with training young. Maybe you want to get an older dog so you can skip the puppy phase and the housetraining and all the chewing and headaches that come with having a pup. There are a lot of good Bloodhounds in the world that need forever homes. A lot of hounds are surrendered or rehomed because owners didn't research the breed and are at their wits' end, or the hound didn't mesh well with their family. One of the biggest reasons hounds get surrendered is because the owner did not fully anticipate the time and energy and dedication it would take to raise a Bloodhound. Whether you want a pup or want to adopt an older dog, there are plenty of them out there just waiting to be the amazing companion they are destined to be.

Buying, Rescuing, or Adopting

Photo Courtesy of
Nancy Boerner
Boerner's Bloodhounds

Determining what you want your dog to do is a big consideration when deciding what age of pup you want to get. If you are looking for a family pet that is a little bit mellower and laid back, you may want to consider getting an older dog. Rescuing a dog that's four or five years old can help you get past the puppy years and get a dog that has burned some of that young energy and wants to live the rest of their life out in relative peace. Just keep in mind, the idea of a Bloodhound that just lies around all day is a bit of an exaggeration as they do have lots of energy throughout life. But older dogs do in fact take more time to enjoy the good things in life like naps and cuddles. Remember that if you go this route, you may still have to spend significant time training as you don't know what their previous environment or level of training is. You may be starting from square one in achieving behaviors you want in an older hound. The saying "You can't teach an old dog new tricks," while being mostly false, will prove to have kernels of truth when it comes to a stubborn breed like Bloodhounds. They will require just as much attention and consistent training as a pup, but maybe in different areas.

If you want a Bloodhound that is going to do what they are designed to do by having them hunt, track, or assist in search and rescue, you will probably want to get a puppy from a reputable breeder. By getting a pup, you will be able to start training them at a young age and start encouraging good behaviors, while discouraging the bad. Basically, you will be able to groom that dog to suit your specific needs. Bloodhounds love to cuddle and be family dogs, but they also love to work. They say that a tired hound is a happy hound, so putting them to work will increase the satisfaction in their own lives and in their owner's lives.

NOT-SO-FUN FACTS
Consider Rescue

Sadly, many people have no idea how much exercise Bloodhounds really need or just how much they drool. That means there are quite a few Bloodhounds in need of rescue or adoption. Consider rescuing a Bloodhound rather than getting a puppy.

Photo Courtesy of Michelle Mantilla

Researching Breeders

By selecting a breeder with championship bloodlines, you can see what previous generations of Bloodhounds have done. You will be able to talk to the breeder about certain behaviors or health ailments that exist in that bloodline and can curtail your puppy selection to those that best suit your needs. If you want to show your dog at dog shows, then it's probably best to pick a breeder who has bred their dogs to be of a high show quality. If you want a working dog, you want to choose a breeder who has experience in breeding working dogs and tracking dogs. These are, of course, just recommendations. My dog came from a breeder who supplies dogs to primarily law enforcement in my state. His sense of smell is acute, and he is built for endurance, but I got him to be a house dog. That has come with its own set of challenges as I had to learn to harness some of the energy he wants to put into tracking and redirect it so he can fulfill his needs and fit into my lifestyle as well.

Once you've decided what you want your dog to do and whether you want a pup or an older dog, it's time for the last step before bringing a slobber monster home. It's time to figure out where you're going to get them from. If, like most people, you're going to start off with a brand new puppy, it's time to start looking for breeders. Finding the right breeder can be a test within itself as some puppy mills and irresponsible people who are just looking for a profit can disguise themselves as reputable breeders. Unethical breeding practices exist in the world and it's important to stay diligent so that you get what you pay for. Bloodhounds are expensive, with champion bloodlines costing well in excess of $2,000. So be patient and do your research. Make sure when you find breeders in your area that they show a true respect and reverence for the breed. Ensure they are professionals and that the dogs they have look good. Ask to see their AKC or registration papers. A lot of backyard breeders will not be able to provide documentation or will give you the run-around. Ask to come to see their dogs and puppies in their environment. This will allow you to see the temperament of the parents and other pups and will also allow you to see the conditions the pups are being raised in. Most reputable breeders take pride in their bloodlines and will gladly show off all the hard work and dedication they have put into creating their line.

Depending on which state you are in, finding a breeder locally may prove difficult. Connecting with breeders on Facebook can be beneficial as you can see past generations and will many times be able to see recommendations and reviews from other people who have adopted from them. Many breeders will offer to ship pups for a fee. My recommendation would be to avoid this if at all possible as it can cause some undue stress on the young pup and your goal should be to make the pup's transition into your family as seamless and stress free as possible. After all, you're starting your relationship with this pup as its owner and leader, and you want your pup to trust that you are going to take care of them from the start.

Researching Rescues

Many people decide to forgo the breeder route and look for dogs at a rescue. Rescues could range from local humane societies to groups that rescue certain breeds like Bloodhounds. Many of the same factors go into choosing a good rescue as with picking a breeder. You want to make sure you are picking a responsible group that has the animal's well-being and health as its utmost priority. Some rescues will specialize in at-risk dogs, which are dogs that may have had incidents in the past that have labeled them as aggressive or unfriendly.

The good part is a lot of rescues take in dogs out of compassion and not for monetary purposes. This means they have the expertise and dedication to seeing the good in dogs that may have had a different future had they not stepped in to rescue them. A lot of rescues can assess a dog's temperament and identify the type of owner and environment that dog will need to be successful. A lot of rescues for Bloodhounds require an in-depth interview process. So if you go this route, be prepared to show that your home and lifestyle are suitable for having a Bloodhound. Home visits and reference interviews are commonplace through a lot of rescues to ensure the dog will have support and access to any special needs.

Rescues are usually more cost effective than buying from a breeder as you will be starting with a dog that has already had other experiences in life that you may need to overcome. Also, rescues have a goal of giving dogs a forever home after a life of uncertainty and sometimes abuse. It's said that there are no bad dogs, just bad owners. So if you decide to get a dog from a rescue, leave your judgments at the door because many of the dogs you will see have the potential to be great pets, but had a tough shot at life before they met you.

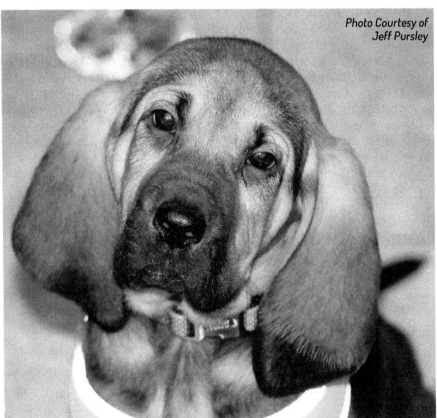

Photo Courtesy of Jeff Pursley

Health Tests and Bloodline Certifications

If you go the route of getting a dog from a rescue or humane society, you may not have access to its health records or genetic predispositions. Bloodhounds have some common health ailments that they are susceptible to no matter what, but if you go through a breeder, you can usually get an idea of what particular ailments affect that bloodline. Some lines are more susceptible to bloat, which is a gastrointestinal ailment that can be life-threatening to dogs. Certain kinds of cancers can also be more prevalent in some bloodlines. Ask your breeder for information on any health concerns that exist with the pup's parents or littermates. Most the time, these health certifications won't be a deciding factor in whether to get a dog from that breeder, but will serve as a way for you to know what to expect and allow you to begin planning on preventative care for your hound.

When you get your pup, most breeders will also provide documentation from the AKC, or American Kennel Club. These documents will allow you to know that your dog was given the utmost care from gestation to birth to rearing. Those documents will also allow access to health certifications where the bloodline has been checked for certain common conditions associated with the breed. With Bloodhounds, the AKC does a hip examination, elbow evaluation, and cardiac exam. These certificates will give you a heads-up on the propensity your dog has to some of these conditions. Most the time, your dog's papers will come with thirty-day pet insurance and the ability to register your dog with the AKC to gain access to full bloodlines and other important information. In all, the AKC paperwork you receive with your pup will allow you to learn everything you can about their familial history and how to provide them with the best life possible.

Things to Consider if Rescuing/Adopting

"If getting a dog from a rescue, chances are that it is an adult. This is when meeting the dog is most important. And try to get as much info on the Bloodhound and why he/she is being re-homed."

Nancy Boerner
Boerner's Bloodhounds

Whether you decide to adopt or rescue a Bloodhound, it is the first step in joining the family of other Bloodhound owners. If you decide to rescue, you can be assured that you are providing a good life to a dog that may not have had the best upbringing. You are its savior, and are showing how

FUN FACT

AKC Ranking

Bloodhounds are the 50th most popular breed registered with the American Kennel Club (AKC).

truly compassionate you are by giving the dog a second chance at life. If you buy or adopt a puppy, you have the responsibility of continuing the long tradition of raising one of the most useful dogs in the animal world. Puppies come with their own struggles, but they are well worth it. Watching your pup grow from a little baby that can fit into your arms to a big, strong, determined dog that can track a week-old scent is truly rewarding. Either way, welcome to the family. We have plenty of support groups and you'll probably need them.

CHAPTER 5
Start Strong With Your Pup

Set Expectations with Family Members

Having a puppy in your home is very similar to having a human baby. All sorts of lifestyle adjustments will need to be made and decisions will abound in how to best take care of them. Where they will sleep, where they will go to the bathroom, and what kind of food to feed them are just a few of the things to consider. A puppy is going to require a lot of time. You are now the one teaching them everything they need to know.

A lot of breeders will start allowing their pups to be adopted around eight weeks old, and the puppies should already be eating solid foods and have an introduction into potty training. But one thing to remember is that this pup has been around its mother and littermates since it was born, so it may start feeling a little lonely and cry out for attention. It will be important to

provide a safe place for your Bloodhound and to be supportive to their growth and development. When they are pups, they will begin finding their voice. And when a Bloodhound finds their voice, they use it a lot. In the beginning they will probably whine and cry as that is what they've done in the past to get their mother's attention. This can be a trying time as the pup will most likely keep you up at night as it cries out for attention, but with strong and consistent training, a restful night's sleep will again be in your future. This chapter will outline some of the things you need to know and get to make your Bloodhound's transition into your home as seamless and stress free as possible.

Photo Courtesy of
Francesca DelSignore

Prepare Your Home and Get the Essentials

We've talked about some of the preparation you'll need to do to get your home in tip-top shape for life with a big dog. Likewise, there will be some items you will need to get to prepare for life with a puppy. Probably the most important will be puppy pads. These will save your floor from unwanted accidents. While your dog is housetraining, accidents will be common, so invest in plenty of paper towels and puppy pads. You can begin by putting a pad down where you want the puppy to go to the bathroom.

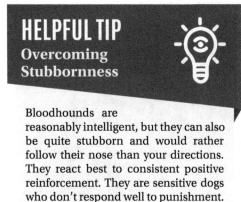

HELPFUL TIP

Overcoming Stubbornness

Bloodhounds are reasonably intelligent, but they can also be quite stubborn and would rather follow their nose than your directions. They react best to consistent positive reinforcement. They are sensitive dogs who don't respond well to punishment.

Even with your best laid plans of trying to get a pup to go in the right spot, odds are they won't. Be ready to clean up poop and pee on a regular basis. Ask family members for help and set expectations with children in the home that this is normal. It may be a great time to start giving young children some responsibility and give them a chance to have a hand in raising the puppy.

While you may have the best intentions of getting your pup to go in the right spot, they will relieve themselves wherever they see fit until they can begin gaining some bladder control. It is usually a good idea to confine your pup to a certain area of the house so that you can keep an eye on where they are going to the bathroom. This will also prevent accidents from going unseen and causing the need for costly repairs or remediation to get smells and stains off the floor.

One way to confine a dog is by use of a baby gate. These can be bought at most stores and will be a good way to keep your puppy confined to the area you want them to be. By having a baby gate to restrict your pup to certain parts of the home, you can also make sure that area is free of dangers and harmful items. For me, I kept the pup close to a door that went to the backyard. This way, when an accident did happen, I could pick up the pup and take him outside to show him the right place to go. I was also able to help train other people in the home not to leave items they didn't want chewed up or ruined in the area where the puppy was. Shoes, socks, and small toys weren't allowed where the puppy was to avoid any harm to the puppy and also harm to household members' belongings. By taking these things into consideration, you will be able to start creating a secure and safe environment for your pup to spend the start of their lives with you.

What to Expect the First Night

Photo Courtesy of Chelsea Amann

Now that you've picked out a spot for your puppy to call their own, and prepared your family for what to expect, it's time for your pup to sleep through the night. This is going to be a tough time for pup and parent as your puppy will most likely cry and whine quite a bit. After all, they are used to having their brothers and sisters around to keep them company. They will be in a new environment and there will be all sorts of new sounds and smells. Get your puppy a comfortable bed to sleep on, but be prepared for it to get chewed up. The pup will be active at all hours and will look for anything to play with.

This is also a good time to start crate training if that's the route you want to go down. Get a crate or cage that the pup can be placed in at night. This will achieve a couple goals. It will begin a routine of letting your pup know when to calm down and sleep and will start the arduous journey of potty training. Dogs don't like to sleep where they go to the bathroom. So while complete potty training is still a long way off, this will begin the process of getting pup to understand that different areas are for different things.

Another benefit of a crate will be to give the pup somewhere secure where they can't get into any trouble. It's easy to fall into the trap of letting your dog sleep with you, because they are so darn cute after all. I tried this the first night I had my Bloodhound. Everything went great for about an hour. The pup was tired after playing and exploring its new home. At one point, right as I started drifting off to sleep, I was woken up by my pup deciding it was time to potty. Right on my face. Now maybe he was just marking his territory because he knew I was going to be his lifelong friend and owner, but most likely it was because he was a puppy and just couldn't hold it. Stay strong and keep your pup in a safe, confined area at night for the first few weeks. The whining and crying will slowly decrease. And while it's heartbreaking and tempting to go in and console your new pup, you'll be doing them a favor by creating a routine where they can feel safe and confident and begin to sleep through the night.

Choosing a Vet You Can Trust

After you've survived the first couple of long, sleepless nights with your new puppy, it's time to start getting other things ready for them to have a happy life in your home. Just like a child needs a doctor, your pup is going to need a veterinarian. Not only will your pup need shots, spaying or neutering, and other care, it will inevitably get into some things that will make you question its safety. This could be anything from your pup swallowing things it's not supposed to, to strange behaviors you weren't expecting. This is where you start shopping for vets that are familiar with your breed. It may be tough finding a vet with a ton of experience in Bloodhounds as they are not as common of a breed as others. General vets will do things like shots and sterilization if you choose to do it, but they may not have the experience in some of the nuances of Bloodhounds in particular.

Finding a good vet is important to set yourself up for success in identifying some of the things you should try to avoid with your dog. Also, they can give more insight into things like when to spay or neuter your dog to ensure you don't stunt their growth, or if tacking their stomach is something they would recommend to prevent bloat. Finding a vet that is familiar with your breed can be tricky, but you can always go back to your breeder and ask who they use. Seeing as how they have probably had to take their dogs in for checkups, they may have some recommendations

Photo Courtesy of Terri Senecal

Photo Courtesy of
Kendall Alguire

of vets or even Bloodhound groups and resources in your area that can give recommendations. The other option is to go the old-fashioned route of calling up local vets and shopping around. Ask if they have any experience with the breed and if they'd feel comfortable treating your dog. Once you have found a vet that suits your needs and is dedicated to the healthcare of your dog, you can rest easier at night knowing you have someone else on your side making sure your pup will start strong in life.

Puppy Food

"Bloodhound puppies drink a lot. Don't be concerned if you are always refilling their water bowl."

Brenda Olive
Hickory Ridge Kennel

One of the things you can do once you find a vet is ask them for recommendations on pet food. There is a whole slew of puppy foods on the market ranging from inexpensive to wallet busting. Speak with your vet about what they recommend for your particular dog. Maintaining a healthy weight and providing the nutrients they need to grow is important in their formative years. Since Bloodhounds are going to grow by leaps and bounds in their first year, they will eat a lot. Dogfoodadvisor. com provides reviews and safety warnings on all sorts of different dog foods and is a great resource to determine if the cheap bag of food from your local grocery store is suitable, or if you should spend a little more at a pet store for premium food. My breeder recommended the Blue Diamond line of food. They make brand name foods for sale at many pet stores and while expensive, they have been recommended to me by multiple sources.

Your puppy should be switched to solid food as soon as possible to ensure they are getting all the nutrients they need to grow their bones and coat. Sometimes soft, canned food can be used to supplement a diet, but kibble is generally considered best for your growing pup. Some people will also swear by a diet of raw foods. Meats, eggs, vegetables, and other proteins can be great if you know what you are doing. But as with all things, moderation and diversity should be key in providing your dog with a healthy diet. The best bet for selecting a food for your dog is talking to your vet so they can recommend a diet that is suitable for your dog's specific dietary needs. Keep in mind that your pup is going to eat a lot and as they grow older, their appetite will grow as well, with many owners saying they feed their dogs 6-8 cups of food a day. So be mindful when selecting a food and buy within your means. Even though a brand may be touted as the absolute best, there are other less expensive brands out there that can provide your pup with everything they need to grow into happy and healthy dogs.

CHAPTER 6
The Joys of Having a Fur Toddler

Staying Strong and Dedicated to Your Goals

Photo Courtesy of
Robyn Griffin-Mixan

You've already overcome some of the biggest hurdles in starting off with your Bloodhound so give yourself a pat on the back. You made a responsible decision on where to get your pup and have set up your house and family members for success. And while you deserve major kudos for getting this far, the fun has only just begun. Now that you've made it through the first night, and hopefully survived without waking up to a warm and wet surprise like I did, it's time to start molding and training your pup into the loyal and obedient dog they will grow to be.

This chapter will focus on a lot of the typical baby Bloodhound behaviors and will provide some tips and tricks on how to curb them before they get out of control. Remember, your hound is going to grow by leaps and bounds, and if some of these behaviors are left unchecked, they could turn into big problems that will be harder to rein in later on. The best advice is to stay strong, stay consistent, and don't let their adorable faces fool you. Even when young, Bloodhounds are already learning how to manipulate their owners and developing their hardheadedness. By staying positive and maintaining focus, you will be able to raise a hound that is a pleasure to be around for your family and your guests.

Crate Training

I've already talked about it a couple times before, but I'm going to again stress the importance of crate training your Bloodhound. At first, I was a huge opponent of crate training. I felt that a dog shouldn't be confined in a cage and thought that I could train him well enough to be trusted outside of his crate when unattended. After multiple chewed up couch cushions, a slew of pee stains on the carpet, and more than a few nights awoken by strange sounds and bangs coming from somewhere in the house, I have changed my tune on how important crate training is. As stated above, the crate gives your dog a safe place to call their own. It allows you to create a routine by giving the dog a cue of when they should calm down or go to bed. It will eventually get to the point where your Bloodhound will go to their crate on their own to take a nap or hang out if they are stressed. The crate can also save your furniture and carpets from unwanted pee stains and assist in potty training. At times it will seem easy to throw your hound in their crate as a punishment, but really you want to avoid this so as not to ruin the perception the dog has of the crate. You want it to remain a happy and inviting place for them so it can continue to be a huge asset in their training.

When looking for crates, look for one that is going to be big enough for your hound. They could stand as high as 27 inches when fully grown, so make sure it's big enough to accommodate them as they grow. I use a crate that is made of wire on all sides with a plastic pan in the bottom. This type of crate will usually come with removable barriers that you can place inside the crate to adjust the size. This will become important as the dog begins to venture further into potty training because they don't like going to the bathroom where they sleep. Of course, as they're young, accidents will happen and they can usually only hold their bladders for an hour per month of age, up to eight hours. But in the meantime, make sure your dog has room to stand up comfortably in their crate without hunching over too much. They should also be able to turn around or spin in their crate.

Also invest in some sort of soft pillow or blanket for the crate, but don't spend too much. Odds are it will end up getting chewed on and torn up. Due to their large size, Bloodhounds will put a lot of weight on their elbows and knees, and if the surface they are lying on is too hard, it will create calluses over time. Avoid that by giving them something soft to lie on since they will be spending nights and other times in their crate. Just keep in mind that we want to create a welcoming place the hound wants to go to soothe themselves, and not to use it as a punishment cage.

Correction Collars

HELPFUL TIP
100-Pound Toddlers

Bloodhounds will follow their nose into a variety of problematic situations, eating things they shouldn't and "counter surfing" to eat anything they can reach. When you have a Bloodhound, you need to essentially baby-proof your home to withstand a four-foot-tall, 100-pound toddler! This will help prevent trips to the emergency vet to remove foreign objects or deal with accidental poisonings.

The next tool I'm going to mention may be met with some criticism, but has been invaluable to me in raising and training my hound. As my pup started to grow and I found it harder and harder to wrangle him, I started researching correction collars. Some people refer to these as shock collars or E-collars, and while they can be abused if not used correctly, they can also provide some much needed reinforcement and correction for your pup. One problem with Bloodhounds is they have an incredibly high pain tolerance. If you couple that with the loose skin all over their body, correction through other methods can seem ineffective. Correction collars have their place with outdoor and tracking training as well, but can also be used within your home to reinforce or discourage certain behaviors.

If you decide to go this route, I recommend buying a collar that has an audible tone and a vibrate function. For me, my hound responds to the vibration on his collar more than any shock, and when paired with the audible tone, I can usually correct any behavior by simply reminding him with a beep. This will help immensely when training your dog on walks but also when they get indignant in your home and push boundaries. A gentle reminder that the vibration or shock stimulus is coming will help keep your dog in control. My hound will start pushing his luck by engaging in behaviors I've trained him not to do, and by simply introducing the collar and placing it around his neck, the behaviors stop and he knows he's out of chances. Again, I don't recommend using the collar as a punishment and it should absolutely not be left on for long periods of time, but it can be an invaluable tool in harnessing some of your large dog's raw energy and indignation.

Chewing

Even though we can try as hard as we can to prevent and correct bad behaviors before they start, puppies are just figuring out how the world works and will lack most impulse control. This means they will inevitably chew on anything that happens to find itself in front of their mouth. Any leftover articles of clothing, toys, and furniture will be prime targets. While the chewing can't necessarily be stopped outright, there are ways to limit it. The main way you're going to be able to limit your pup's chewing is by just paying attention to them and not leaving them unattended for long periods of time. By keeping an eye on them, you will be there to provide instant correction when the dog starts chewing.

Some people employ spray bottles as a way to correct the behavior and stop the chewing. This won't always work because a lot of Bloodhounds LOVE water, so then they'll just be chewing on your couch and cooling off at the same time. Another option would be some sort of chewing deterrent that you can buy at your local pet store. The sprays are usually non-toxic, but are made of something bitter that will leave a bad taste in the dog's mouth if they try. Of course, make sure you read the warning labels on those sprays and before spraying it on anything, check for colorfastness as some of these sprays can stain or discolor furniture and carpet.

The last good chewing deterrent is making sure you have plenty of toys for the pup. Essentially you want to distract them with things they are allowed to chew on so that they don't eat things they aren't supposed to chew on. But, no matter how many toys or sprays you get, a puppy is going to chew on items left on the floor. So just be mindful that they are learning how to exist in their new environment and are very much like human toddlers who just wander around sticking whatever they find in their mouths.

Growling, Barking, and Food Aggression

As puppies grow and learn what is right and wrong, you will more than likely have to focus some time on making sure your pet is not aggressive around food. Coming from a pack environment, they are probably used to fending off their littermates for whatever scraps of food they can get their little paws on. They communicate to others to back off by growling and showing their teeth. This can be concerning as we want to make sure our pups are friendly and not a threat to small children or

Photo Courtesy of
Lindsey Norman

other household pets. That's why it is important to control this behavior whenever it pops up.

One way to show a puppy that you are in control is to take their food bowl and place it in front of you. Pretend that you are eating out of it and then, only after you have shown that you ate first, give it to your pup. This helps establish your role as alpha in the pack and shows that they cannot show aggression toward you. Most food aggression is just harmless posturing, but should be taken seriously as a bite can have serious consequences.

Another way to combat food aggression is to feed your pup one kernel of kibble at a time from your hand. This will teach them to be gentle since you can correct them if your fingers get nibbled. This method again shows the dog that you are in control of the food and that they will eat only when you say it's okay. Make sure that you, as the adult, test the dog's limits and identify its aggression, because a lot of kids won't be as mindful of the dog's space and could easily find themselves in a situation where they have the potential to be bitten. Get close to your dog, bother them a bit, keep testing and correcting so that you can make sure your dog has good tableside manners.

Anxiety

Now that your pup is beginning to learn how to behave inside your home, it's also a good time to start training them to know what's acceptable in the yard. Bloodhounds are sensitive creatures. They can be extremely skittish when it comes to new things introduced in their environment. Some of these items may seem mundane, like yard tools or bird feeders, but some may pose a perceived threat to your Bloodhound. It's not uncommon to hear a commotion coming from your yard as your Bloodhound witnesses people working on a neighbor's house, or, in my case, a hot air balloon floating over a couple miles away.

Most dogs will alarm their owners to occurrences that are out of the ordinary, so this in itself isn't that uncommon. The issue many Bloodhound owners will experience is that the Bloodhound will remember this situation and be wary of the area for days or weeks to come. One time a neighbor of mine set a ladder on the side of their house. My hound saw it, started baying, and would not stop. Every time I let him out after that, he would slink over to that side of the house and start sniffing like crazy trying to identify if the object was still there. There was a solid week where he wouldn't venture out from under the patio awning because he had seen a hot air balloon flying over and developed a fear that there was inevitably more coming.

Photo Courtesy of April Conklin

The reason it's important to know how wary Bloodhounds can be of their environment is because it can help us understand some of their behaviors that may happen because of their anxiety. Believe it or not, Bloodhounds can develop anxiety due to things or situations that they are not used to in their environment. This anxiety can lead to all sorts of different behaviors. If your dog is scared of something outside, they may start peeing in the house after being potty trained. They can also start one of the worst Bloodhound behaviors of digging. Since Bloodhounds are so strong, they are master diggers. They will dig their paws in and dig tunnels and holes in any soft part of dirt they can find. This can be entirely frustrating as they will seek out any freshly disturbed dirt and dig it up. Remember the potatoes I mentioned before? They were in the ground for less than five minutes before my hound dug them up. Not only is this concerning as it has the potential to undo all your hard work you put into your landscaping, but also because bath time usually has to follow these excavation incidents. A lot of times, anxiety can be blamed for digging.

Digging

If your dog is nervous outside, or scared of something, bad behaviors will oftentimes present themselves as an outlet for that pent-up energy. Of course, digging can also be attributed to boredom or not enough exercise. So make sure to get your hound some toys, walk them frequently, and do all you can to create a safe and inviting environment for them. If they do start digging, try to identify what the root cause of their anxiety or outburst could possibly be. By identifying the external stressor they are experiencing, you can better understand and stop the negative behaviors that have you pulling your hair out in frustration.

Routines and How They Help Your Pup

Combatting the behaviors listed above can seem like a daunting task. Pair that with the sheer size and stubbornness of your Bloodhound and it may seem downright impossible. But the biggest advice I can give to overcome these hurdles is to remain consistent and attentive to your dog. Try to understand their natural demeanor. By gaining a grasp of how and why your dog is the way they are, you can learn how to train them and support them to grow into loyal and obedient pets. Stay consistent and try to create a routine through crate training and positive reinforcement so that your dog understands your expectations. After all, starting strong with your pup now will save you from hours of frustration, unnecessary landscaping projects, and tons of home repairs down the road.

CHAPTER 7
Getting them to "Go" When and Where You Want Them To

"When house training, be consistent and use positive reinforcement. Take them outside when first waking up, or immediately following eating, drinking or playing. Praise them and give treats for going outside. But most of all have patience!"

Heather Pearson
Black Diamond Bloodhounds & Bracco Italianos

Expectations for Potty Training

The following subject is probably the hardest for me to speak about as it was the single most difficult thing I had to teach my Bloodhound. Potty training other dog types has usually been a breeze. It comes with its own struggles and there is definitely a need to be patient, but those experiences could never have prepared me for what I went through with my Bloodhound. Some of it may be attributed to their stubbornness while some may be blamed on posturing in the pack, but no matter what the reason, having a dog refuse to be potty trained can be the biggest test you face as a pet owner.

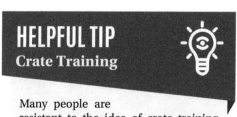

HELPFUL TIP
Crate Training

Many people are resistant to the idea of crate training their dogs, but a dog that is properly crate trained doesn't see it as a punishment. Even if you don't plan on keeping your Bloodhound in a crate when you leave the house, he may encounter kennels at the vet, groomer, or boarding facility, and you owe it to your pup to teach him to be comfortable in a crate or kennel.

The implications from your pup going in the wrong spot can be overwhelming. A pup that's not potty trained can easily ruin carpets, hardwood floors, grass lawns, and anything else lying on the floor. Some accidents are bound to happen when a pup is young and that is to be expected. But trust me, without

dedication, supervision, and constant reinforcement, potty training troubles can continue well past your dog's first year and will strain the relationship you have with them. So learn from my mistakes, and allow all the research I've done on this topic to be a guide to help you avoid the nightmare of a pup that refuses to go where you want them to go.

To start things off, it's important to go into this battle with the proper expectations of what your Bloodhound is capable of and what you should realistically expect them to be able to do. When your pup is young, they will inevitably have accidents. Not only are their bladders smaller so they can't physically hold their urine for long periods, but they are just starting off and are just gaining a grasp of how to control their behavior. It's for this reason that I'd recommend not leaving your pup unsupervised much without them being confined to a crate or delegated area.

As your pup grows, it's realistic to expect them to be able to hold their urine for about an hour for every month old they are. This limit maxes out at eight hours, but is a good rule to help you know what your dog is capable of. It means that for the first couple months, you will be making many, many trips outside with your dog and will be investing heavily in cleaning supplies and clean-up rags. Your local pet store sells puppy pads that will absorb any accidents in the house, but the problem is getting your pup to learn to go on them. If you are going to put the time into training them to go in a certain place, it might as well be going outside where they will be going in adulthood. We'll discuss some of the products out there to help with getting your dog to go in a certain location, but the most important technique comes from within you as the owner.

Techniques

The technique that will benefit you the most while potty training your Bloodhound is going to be positive reinforcement. We will talk about conditioning, reinforcement, and punishment later, but for now, let's focus on positive reinforcement. In other words, you want to reward your hound for what they do right, instead of punishing them for what they do wrong. This may seem counterintuitive at times, because everything in you is going to want to yell and punish your dog for peeing on the floor or on your favorite pair of shoes, but in the end, it's pointless.

First off, Bloodhounds have a huge pain tolerance, so any of the traditional methods you see, like rolling up a newspaper and swatting them on the nose, won't work. In fact, Bloodhounds can turn aggressive when challenged or exposed to pain, so finding another route to train through is your best bet. Second, you have to understand that Bloodhounds really do have fragile psyches. They love to be told they are doing a good job, and punishment or scolding can actually push them deeper into a stubborn mindset. It's almost as if they start beating themselves up for doing a bad job, and then just dwell on that, becoming more stubborn and misbehaving as time goes on. I've noticed with my hound that negativity will have no effect on him in conditioning or training, whereas over-the-top, boisterous praise does. So practice your happy voice. Make sure you have a big smile. Get those belly rubs ready. Your pup, and your floors, will thank you for it later.

Rewarding and Praise for a Job Well Done

Making a big deal out of your dog's accomplishments is hands down the best motivator in creating good behaviors. And even though it's extremely important, praise alone is usually not enough to help you overcome the hurdle of potty training. Other tools and products exist in the world to help make training your dog a breeze. One of the most common is a bell of some sort that goes by the back door where you want your dog to go outside. Some bells can be screwed in to the door frame and others can be hung from a string that's tied to the knob. It really depends on what fits your home. The important part is getting a bell that your dog can ring when they need to go out. The ultimate goal is for them to go over to the door and ring the bell on their own to signal they need to go out. Kim Dillon from Sandstone Kennels also encourages this technique and says, "The puppy will eventually know to nudge the bell when they need to go outdoors."

Training them to do this is easy enough, and a good intro to operant conditioning. When your pup is young, they will definitely have an accident in the house. Rather than getting mad and rubbing their nose in it, try calmly picking them up, take them to the door, ring the bell and put them outside. After they have been outside, put on that excited face and congratulate them and praise them. Tell them what a good dog they are and give them extra love. Bloodhounds are especially motivated by attention, so it can be a great way to train them. You can use treats to reward them after going outside too, but eventually you want them to do it without expecting a treat. And if they know they are going to get food out of the deal, they may start going to the door and ringing the bell because they know it will produce food. Try using love and adoration as it will be more effective on your dog and cost less in the long run.

Supervising Your Pup to Stay Consistent

I wish that it could always be as easy as staying calm and just rewarding your dog, but when it comes to potty training, it's important to stay realistic. Times are going to happen when it seems like no matter how hard you're trying, your hound just won't go where you want them to. Frustration will kick in and it will be very hard not to punish them for doing their business where they aren't supposed to. The hardest part of this will be when you find accidents and weren't there to see them happen. Conditioning won't necessarily work after the fact, so it's important to remember that supervision is key. If you find poop or pee after the deed has been done and don't catch them in the act, try not to get too mad. We're trying to change the behavior of the pup, so punishing them later when they are doing something else will just confuse them. While they are young, keep an eye on them so that when they start to squat or lift their leg, you can stop them in the act. When you catch them doing the deed, redirect them outside and put them in the spot they are supposed to go. Follow up with praise. Don't leave them unsupervised or free to roam in those first few months if you want to get ahead of their housetraining. Be there and be consistent to help condition them to go where they are supposed to. Female dogs seem to be easier to train as males will want to mark territory if they are not neutered. But even then, there are tips and tricks to help male dogs find a spot to claim as their own.

For male dogs, lifting their leg can easily become an obsession. And with Bloodhounds, their noses help them pick up on any foreign smell and cause them to want to mark their territory. They will often pee on anything that is standing upright. For this reason, you can pick up dif-

Photo Courtesy of April Conklin

ferent products at your local pet store to put in your yard outside to get them to pee where you want them to. There are garden stakes, fake rocks, and sprays that can be used to signal to the dog where they should go. I've heard some people say having a human male mark a spot in the backyard will achieve the same goal, and while I have tried it, I did not see a long-term benefit from this technique.

My saving grace was a leash and persistence. When I'd let my pup outside, I'd put him on a leash and walk him over to the area I wanted him to use. I'd then wait for him to do his business, and then congratulate him in a loud and excited tone followed by lots of love and adoration. It took some time, but before long I was able to let him out on his own, and he'd go over to that area. Besides showing him where to go, using his waste against him also worked. I called it poo warfare. Dogs really don't like eating, sleeping, or playing where they use the restroom. So I would scatter some of his toys around parts of the yard where I didn't want him to pee or poop. This caused him to find somewhere else to go so his precious toys didn't turn into unintended casualties of war.

Using his crate also helped in potty training. Again, dogs don't like sleeping where they go to the bathroom, so they will try to avoid it at all costs. When they are young, accidents are going to happen because they simply can't hold it overnight. But as they grow, they will start showing restraint when in their crate. The biggest consideration to take in is to get a crate large enough for your dog to stand up in. If the crate is too big, they may have the ability to go to the bathroom on one side of it, while sleeping on the other. Mine did this, and he'd cover it up with a blanket afterward so he didn't have to look at it. Because of this, if you go down the crate training route, make sure the crate isn't too big. Many will come with dividers or partitions so you can keep the crate at just the right size

CHAPTER 7 Getting them to "Go" When and Where You Want Them To

for your pup so they aren't crowded but also don't have enough room to use one side as a bathroom.

Use the crate to create consistency and a routine for them as well. Put them in it overnight and then immediately let them out into the yard when you get up in the morning. This will set the expectation with them to hold it knowing that they will be let out at a certain time to go to the bathroom.

By following some of these steps, you can create a routine and instill in your pup good manners about when and where they are supposed to go to the bathroom.

When all is said and done, you've tirelessly trained your Bloodhound when and where to go and done your best to prevent accidents in the house. But remember when I said Bloodhounds were a stubborn breed? That can be especially true when it comes to potty training. It is not uncommon for males to need training well into their second year of life. At times it will seem like they are just being downright defiant. But it's not anything to blame yourself for; I'm sure you did great on training them. They are just hardheaded and aren't the quickest to learn sometimes. Spaying and neutering can help tremendously, as it takes away some of that desire to mark territory.

Keeping Your Home from Smelling Like a Kennel

But no matter what, you're going to want to stock up on household cleaners so that you can make sure your house doesn't smell like a kennel. Hounds in general already have a unique smell to them, so you don't need to add poop or pee to the mix. Get yourself a cleaner specifically made for destroying urine stains and odors. Most of these will have enzymes in them that will break up the molecules in urine that cause it to stink. Some can even be placed in your carpet cleaner, so look at the cleaning products section at your local pet store to see what options would work best for you. With a combination of training, consistency, and plenty of cleaning products, you will be able to keep the dog pee outside, and the clean fresh scent of your home on the inside.

59

CHAPTER 8
Making Friends – Both Human and Canine

"In my opinion, Puppy Kindergarten classes between 12-16 weeks old are a must. If you have farm animals, take your pup out around them on a daily basis and let it know that it is not to run after and chase them. The more exposure the pup has early on, the better the grown dog."

Deborah Thompson
Cyclone Ridge Kennels

Why Socialization is Important

HELPFUL TIP
Socialization

Bloodhounds are generally friendly dogs, but they need lots of socialization as puppies to become truly comfortable meeting new dogs and people without any wariness or suspicion. Take your Bloodhound puppy as many places as possible to get him used to new environments, people, and dogs.

So far, we've been focusing on all the things we need to do to make sure your pup behaves for you at home with your family. It's equally crucial to make sure your Bloodhound is also ready to meet guests and other dogs. Socialization is important for hounds because you want to make sure your dog is friendly and controllable when being introduced to others. With their large size, the last thing you want is your Bloodhound bounding toward a guest who just came into your home and knocking them down. You also want to make sure your dog is not overly aggressive with strangers and doesn't cause problems when you take them out. Bloodhounds can be extremely protective and territorial, especially around kids they view as their own. With that being said, having guests over into your home may present its own challenges as that is the Bloodhound's territory. The main part you want to focus on is making sure your pup gets the socialization they need so you can take them on walks, out in public, or to the dog park without incident.

Teaching Your Pup How to Greet Other People

First of all, there is nothing more valuable in socializing your dog than practice and experience. Start young if at all possible and take them with you when you go out. A lot of pet stores and hardware stores allow dogs and this is a great place to test your dog's limits. Of course, you only want to do this when you are confident that your dog is not aggressive and won't injure anyone or any other dogs. When your dog is a pup, start by taking them out for walks at a nearby park or just around your neighborhood. The beneficial part of this is that because your pup is so adorable and most likely pretty rare, people will undoubtedly want to pet them and approach them. Make sure to encourage this but also lay some ground rules. It's perfectly acceptable to tell the person to hold their hand out first so the dog can smell them first. After all, it's your dog and you know what's best for it. People will be drawn to your dog, so now it's time to make sure your dog behaves as well. The last thing you want is your dog getting too excited and jumping all over them. When my hound was a pup, I made sure to let people know he drools a lot. That way the other person could decide if they still wanted to pet him and be aware that they may fall victim to a slobber bomb.

Photo Courtesy of
Sue Daniel

Photo Courtesy of Kendra Albrecht

When someone asks if they can pet your dog, get your dog under control first. Since they're going to be on a leash, try to make them sit. This will work twofold as your pup will learn to be calm and not jump, and will have that behavior reinforced by getting pets and love from whoever is giving them the attention. Then afterward, make sure to tell your dog what a good job they did. Reinforce the good behaviors, and swiftly correct bad ones. Again, its okay to set ground rules and tell someone who is meeting your dog to wait until you make the dog sit before petting them. Every single interaction will be the foundation for the next, so make sure to take your dog out, socialize them at every chance you get, and encourage good behaviors in your dog and the people who pet it.

Puppy Play Dates: When and Where

Beyond just introducing your Bloodhound to people, you're going to want to make sure your dog meets other dogs, too. Puppy play dates serve many of the same functions as play dates between kids do. It helps with socialization and helps the dog learn a lot of things you as the owner can't teach. Certain aspects of canine behavior have to be introduced by other dogs. Sure, your dog probably spent at least six weeks with its littermates, but a lot of that time was purely instinct and survival. Other dogs will teach your hound many things including pack structure, bite inhibition, and patience.

These play dates should usually occur in a neutral place so you don't run into any dominance issues associated with territory. If you take a dog to someone else's home or vice versa, you are introducing them to someone else's territory and protective or aggressive behaviors can rear their heads. Find a place like a park where you can control your dog and how many other pets are around. Dog parks are great later on, but initially you want to be able to remove your dog if any aggression kicks in. Your pup also needs to build their immunities and get vaccinated against certain canine diseases, so wait on taking them to the dog park until you can be sure they will come out safe and healthy.

Introducing Your Pet to Other People's Pets

Now that you're at a park where you can control your dog in a more one-on-one environment, begin introducing your dog to others. Keep an eye on them because you can never fully trust the training a stranger has put into their dog, but let the dogs smell each other. Quickly into the interaction, one will usually assert dominance and begin sniffing the other's rear end. Encourage your dog that it's okay, pet them, and reinforce the behavior just like you would with any other training.

Let the dogs greet each other like dogs do. Keep them on a secure leash but give them some room to move around. They will most likely start playing, with your pup rolling on its back to submit to the likely bigger dog. The bigger dog will usually assert itself and this is okay as it teaches your pup how to act around other dogs and how to accept its place in the pack. A little bit of play biting is okay, and as a pup is perfectly normal. Older dogs will usually use a paw to put your pup down or make them submit if they bite too hard. Learning how to play is important, but learning how to play nice is more important. Make sure the other owner is being attentive to their dog as well and at the first sign of growling, snarling, raised lips, or aggression, separate the dogs. Then calm your pup down by making them sit and getting them back in control. As time goes on, you will be able to let your dog play without as much supervision because they will learn what's right and wrong from other, more experienced dogs.

Photo Courtesy of
Clive Norman

Photo Courtesy of
Cevin Bosley

Bloodhounds and Small Children

Introducing your dog to other adults and dogs is one thing, but introducing them to kids is a whole different beast. First off, your dog's size is going to be a challenge because they are so big and heavy that they could easily knock most kids over. When your dog's full grown, they will probably dwarf a lot of adults when they stand on their hind legs, so training them to be gentle giants will make everyone's life easier later.

The issue with introducing your hound to kids is that kids usually don't understand a dog's limits. They will want to be all up in your dog's business, pulling on them and getting in their face and a whole myriad of other behaviors that could pester your dog. This is why all the training is important and why you should be testing your dog's limits before ever introducing them to a child. This way you can know beforehand what to warn kids to stay away from. With practice and proper training, Bloodhounds make amazingly loyal and patient family dogs. They have so many folds and flaps and so much loose skin that will get pulled and yanked by kids that it's crucial to prep your dog for it. Spend some time doing all the things that you could imagine a kid doing to your dog. Obviously you want to be gentle with them, but try tugging their tail a bit, lift their lips to look at their teeth. Do all the things a kid may do so that you know how your dog will react when a kid does the same things. Bloodhounds are such large cuddly dogs that kids will naturally want to climb on them and wrestle with them. Be mindful of keeping the children in check also by setting ground rules. After all, kids need to learn how to be gentle with dogs in the same way dogs need to be gentle with them.

Pay attention and be cognizant of your dog's cues when they are getting annoyed. Give them a place to go to get away from the kids in case they're too much for the dog to handle. If any signs of aggression or growling exist, quickly separate the dog from the kids and put the dog in their safe space. More than likely they aren't showing aggression to be mean, but rather as a signal that they are getting hurt or annoyed.

As with all of the things discussed so far in this book, supervision is key. Hold your pup and let the kids approach it slowly. Keep an eye open for cues that the dog is not handling the interaction well. And lastly, don't be afraid to set the ground rules on every interaction. This will ensure your guests, kids, and pup all come out of their meetings unscathed.

CHAPTER 9
Bringing the Wild Into Your Home – A Pack of Your Own

"When meeting another dog in the household, I always suggest introducing them outside in the yard first. There isn't as much confined space for the older dog to feel cornered or threatened by an excited puppy or bloodhound. Always introduce slowly and as gently/calmly as possible. When bringing an adult bloodhound in, I suggest always feeding separately. Bloodhounds tend to be food aggressive with other dogs."

Nancy Boerner
Boerner's Bloodhounds

Photo Courtesy of
Sue Daniel

Understanding the Pack Mentality

It's been discussed that Bloodhounds are great cuddlers and family dogs, but try to remember that they are still animals, and having an animal in your home means you have to play by some of their rules. Dogs in particular have a unique social structure, and by understanding it, you can use some of its constructs to help you establish your Bloodhound's role in your home. Everyone's heard of a wolf pack or the pack mentality, and it's an innate set of rules ingrained in your dog from birth. Even when they are puppies, their place in the pack is quickly determined. A dog's place in the pack will affect its access to resources like food and water. Those higher on the chain are going to have access to more resources, while those lower will have to wait for leftovers.

In new litters, the pack is led by a male and female pair, the father and mother, and they are designated as Alphas. Most of the pups will fall into the next classification within the pack, which is the Beta. They are essentially second in line to everything. Mom and Dad rule the roost, while the pups are all below them in the social structure. Lastly, there is almost always an Omega in the back. They are the lowest of the totem pole and will be the one who struggles most for resources. The Omega is most likely smaller than the rest or has some sort of defect. The runt of the litter is often designated as the Omega.

HELPFUL TIP
Introducing Your Bloodhound to Other Pets

Bloodhounds are generally friendly with other pets and don't often see small animals as prey. However, if you adopt an adult Bloodhound, smaller animals may be intimidated by the new dog's size and their fear could cause them to lash out. Make sure to read everybody's body language when introducing your Bloodhound to other pets.

But just because a dog gets assigned a certain class within the pack doesn't necessarily mean that they are unlucky or will have a harder shot at life. Since the pack mentality is ingrained from birth and almost purely instinctual, the dogs will thrive by knowing their place in the pack, and it's important for owners to reinforce that social structure as to not cause any dissent or confusion amongst other dogs. By understanding that there will always be a leader, those subservient to the leader, and then one at the bottom of the social structure, you can harness the nature of the dog pack and bring it into your home successfully.

Identifying Your Pet's Role in the Pack

Photo Courtesy of Diane Stradling

So how do we go about determining the pecking order in the pack? With one animal, it's fairly straightforward. Humans all share the role of Alpha, regardless of size or age, and your dog is Omega. Don't think about it as designating your dog as second-class, but rather as protecting the people in your family before your dog. If your dog sees itself as higher in the pack than, let's say a child, aggression will emerge and the dog will try to posture itself in a higher standing. This is because the dog will see an opportunity to gain more access to resources like food and attention.

Pack position can be especially difficult to establish with Bloodhounds. When around others of their own kind, nature takes over and things fall into place relatively seamlessly. But when humans are introduced, certain nuances can challenge the pack structure. Since Bloodhounds will grow to be so large, their sheer size can make them think they are in a higher standing than those smaller than them. This means children will be challenged for their spot in the pack. This can be overcome by ensuring your hound knows where they stand by making them sit and watch you give attention to your child. Don't let the hound barge in and demand your time or attempt to get in between your child and you. Maybe even place your hound in their crate while you show love and adoration to your child. Make it obvious that the hound's job is to witness the interaction, to allow those in the family the access to resources first, and to engage or join in only when invited.

We mentioned this with food aggression before. If your hound is showing food aggression, it's because they are challenging the pack structure. By being aggressive, they are trying to show that whoever is approaching has to wait until they are done eating. If that happens, the dog needs to be retrained as to who is Alpha. Feeding the dog one kernel of food at a time from your hand will show that they are submissive to you or whoever is feeding them, and will only get access to food when those higher in pack standing allow it.

As with everything we've mentioned with Bloodhounds, remember that they are stubborn. Things that should be easy to train can be especially difficult due to their hard heads and self-determination. It's not uncommon for Bloodhounds to actually be quite agile and position themselves physically higher than those around them. We'll touch on this a bit later, but one thing Bloodhound owners will often report is "counter surfing." This can start with them standing on their hind legs with their paws up on your counter or table, to them actually physically standing atop a table. If you look at videos online, you will be able to see numerous instances of owners coming home to their Bloodhound standing atop a counter or cabinets and standing proud while doing it. While it may seem confusing and frustrating at first, just know that these behaviors come down to social posturing. Your dog is using their size and physical location to try to assert that they are bigger and therefore more dominant than those around. In other words, they are the king looking down on all the peasants in the house around them. It can be funny and make you shake your head while calling them a goofball, but know that it's important to correct the behavior and not allow it. If your hound gets away with this sort of posturing, they will also begin with other bad behaviors. Ensure they are put in their place, disciplined appropriately, and reassured of their standing in the pack. By understanding the pack structure and how certain behaviors are used for social posturing, you can make sure to correct them and re-establish the natural order within your home.

All these things may be great when spoken aloud, but when put into practice, it may not seem as easy. Getting your Bloodhound to accept you as Alpha can be one of the biggest tasks you will have to take on. Because they are big and can seem scary if they growl or bare their teeth, many owners will often back down to avoid getting bitten. Earlier we talked about how Bloodhounds will grab anything they find on the floor and try to chew it. Getting those items away can lead to tense moments of social posturing. Many times, hounds will take an item and then when their owner tries to get it away, they will growl or show aggression. Obviously, this behavior needs to be eradicated and should not be allowed to happen. If your Bloodhound sees that they can intimidate you into getting what they want, they are in reality asserting dominance and challenging your authority. Since Bloodhounds are so strong and could easily cause some serious damage if that aggression leads to physical violence, many people will shy away from correcting that bad behavior. This is where the things we talked about before need to be reiterated. Start young, while your pup is still relatively easy to control. Be confident and stern in your correction. Don't get mad and yell, as this could have the opposite of the desired effect and make the situation worse. Be stern, and use whatever your tool of choice is to get them to comply and submit to you. For some this would be where an E-collar comes into place. When the dog starts showing aggression, use the collar to assert dominance and remind them that they must listen to you. If you're against an E-collar, you can also use your hound's natural aversion to everyday things to get them to listen. My Bloodhound's kryptonite is a Swiffer. All I need to do is grab it and he will drop what he is doing and retreat to his crate. I never hit him with it, or did anything that would make him learn to hate the Swiffer. But for whatever reason, he decided he hates it, and when he starts to challenge me or anyone else in the house, simply grabbing it from the corner will quickly remind him that we are the ones who are in control.

Bloodhounds and Other Household Animals

After all is said and done and you've established your dog's place in their human pack, you may still have struggles with other pets. As stated above, dogs are more aware of their pack structure amongst each other than we as humans are. So if you have another dog in the home, be mindful of that and observe their dynamic to help things run smoothly. If you have any other pets in your home, you will basically have two packs: a human pack with your dog and family members, and then an animal pack with all your pets included. Most older dogs will automatically assume the

Photo Courtesy of Shyla Bryant

Photo Courtesy of
Lindsey Norman

dominant role, but size can play a role in this. You will be able to notice the pack hierarchy in your home by looking at your dogs' behaviors.

As an easy way to identify how your dogs have lined up in the pack, do a test by getting some treats for them. Usually one dog will approach first and push in front of the other dog. That dog is the Alpha. When you get home, one dog will usually come toward you while one stays behind. There are many behaviors that will present themselves where you will be able to see one dog submit to another.

Options if Pets Don't Get Along

If the dogs aren't getting along or there is aggression between them, it is most likely because there is a power struggle in place. You can try to pay attention to which dog is Alpha and reinforce that standing so the other will learn to submit. Just like we said with kids, you can put the Beta dog in a crate or separate from the Alpha, and then feed the Alpha. Let one dog watch the other get fed first and receive attention from you. Don't worry, this won't breed jealousy or feelings of being inadequate or not being the favorite fur baby. This will just help reinforce the natural pack order and show the Beta that it needs to submit to the Alpha. The dog will pick up on your cues if you've established your place in the pack, and will begin to fall in line and restore a peaceful order in your home.

CHAPTER 10
Exercise – Your Bloodhound's Best Friend

"They need quite a bit of exercise. People tend to think that this is a lazy breed but when we let our Bloodhounds out for their exercise, they are nonstop running around and sniffing every inch of the area where we let them out. We have a dedicated field for our dogs to go outside to get their exercise. I would recommend allowing the dog to go outside multiple times per day. Develop an activity to do with them, of course after they finish sniffing everything out."

Kim Dillon
Sandstone Kennels

Energy Expectations

A lot of the bad behaviors already discussed in this book can be easily avoided with one thing: exercise. One of the familiar adages in Bloodhound life is that "a tired hound is a happy hound." Not only will a tired hound be happy, but they will make you happy because you won't be dealing with bad behaviors brought on by excess energy.

A lot of people have an image in their head of Bloodhounds being lazy dogs that sleep on porches most of the day. This couldn't be further from the truth, especially with young dogs. Bloodhounds are built for endurance. This means they can go and go and go. If they don't have an outlet for all the pent-up energy, they will often turn to destructive behaviors like digging and chewing. Really, exercise will be your dog's best friend. It will help them not only to stay fit and burn energy, but to be able to fit into your life and home. As a puppy, your Bloodhound will be fairly easy to control and will have plenty of space to run around. But as they grow, their space requirements will grow and they will need lots of room to run. It's not only their space requirements that will grow, but they will require a physically strong owner to be able to control them when out on walks.

Walking, Running, and Sometimes Dragging

A Bloodhound's nose drives it above all other instincts. They are meant to follow tracks and scents tirelessly. This will pose some challenges when taking them on walks because they will have a million new things to smell, and will literally drag their owner toward it. It's because of this instinct to track that Bloodhounds should almost always be on a leash when not safe at home. If they are left to run free, they will follow a scent and will stop responding to their owner as they run and track the scent's origin.

The hardest part about walking a Bloodhound is this drive to follow scents, paired with their sheer strength. They will drop low to the ground, and get as much leverage as possible to pull toward wherever the scent is coming from. Kids and people with smaller frames may have a hard time overcoming this strength and can quite literally be dragged while the dog is out for their daily walk. So make sure you can handle your dog's strength and have what it takes to be able to walk them. If you aren't able to handle a hundred-pound dog pulling with all its might in a certain direction, it may be time to reconsider owning this breed. But if you have what it takes to keep control of your hound and have the patience to teach them how to walk right, you will be well on your way to giving them what they need in exercise.

Equipment Needed to Make Walks Enjoyable for All

Photo Courtesy of Makenze Bullins

The way Bloodhounds pull when walked can also cause them to get hurt, so there's some equipment you're going to want to get to make walks easier on you and your hound. The first recommendation is a harness to attach their leash to. This relieves any pressure that's put on their throat that could cause them to choke or damage their windpipe, and places it on their chest. By putting the pressure on your dog's frame, it more evenly distributes the pressure and strain put on their body. A lot of harnesses come with pockets or pouches on the side that can carry items along with you on your walk. These are beneficial in two ways. First of all, they are convenient. You can pack up some bags to pick up poop with and treats for reinforcement when your dog is behaving correctly. Secondly, you can use those pouches to add some weight to the harness. This will cause your hound to walk a bit slower and will provide more work for them to do while walking. Bloodhounds love having a purpose and a job, so when they feel like they are doing something, they put their all into it and gain more satisfaction out of the activity. What putting weight on the harness accomplishes for the owner is that it helps tire the dog out quicker. It can make shorter walks more beneficial and give the dog what they need without having to run around the block ten times over.

Other types of leashes and collars exist for training your dog to walk without pulling, but are not as effective. Some people will swear by pinch collars. These are collars that have prongs all the way around them that, when tightened, will pinch the dog's neck, inflicting a minimal amount of pain. The dog then learns that the less it pulls, the less it will hurt. While these collars have a place in training for some breeds, they present some unique challenges with Bloodhounds. Due to the excess skin around a bloodhound's neck, they may not be able to feel the pressure or slight pain caused by the collar and won't respond to it. Similar to that, the Bloodhound's high pain tolerance and downright determination will make pinch collars less effective at training than with other breeds.

Again, I recommend the E-collar. As you can tell, I use this item almost exclusively in training. The main reason is that when I put it on, my dog knows it's time to work and that he won't get away with any bad behaviors. Also, I feel better about it because I am not hurting my dog while he is simply doing what he was bred to do and following his nose. The collar I use has a beep, vibrate, and shock function. Normally, I can get away with just giving my dog a quick beep, and he knows to redirect his focus. If he continues to misbehave, I will use the vibrate function, which he reacts to incredibly well and will stop him in his tracks. I rarely have had to use the shock function. The only time I used it was to teach my hound the progression of stimulation he would receive for not following commands. It's important to test the shock out on yourself and if you think it hurts, then it's probably too strong for the dog. Adjust it to a point where it gets their attention, but does not inflict pain.

Photo Courtesy of
Lindsey Norman

Regardless of what technique you use, just know it will take time, patience, and practice to get your dog to fully obey on walks and stop pulling toward the scents they come across. After all, the breed has been selectively designed to make them do exactly that, so overcoming it is a challenge but well worth it and necessary if you ever hope to control your Bloodhound.

Other Forms of Physical Exercise

Beyond just walking your dog, you may want to find other activities to wear them out. They have seemingly unending energy when they are young, and trips to doggy day care or dog parks may be a nice addition to your exercise regimen. If you are able and willing, doggy day cares offer some advantages to getting your dog the exercise they need. They will have the opportunity to play with other dogs, smell new environments, and spend the day expending built-up energy rather than being confined to a crate or dog run. Dog parks offer the same opportunity for getting the energy out and can definitely be supplemented to get your dog moving.

The problem with dog parks is that you don't know how other people have trained their dogs. Pack mentality and posturing can kick in and depending on how other people have trained their dogs, scary fights can

*Photo Courtesy of
Kailyn Evans
Kailyn Evans Photography*

*Photo Courtesy of
Ashley and Spencer Hall*

occur. Most of the time, dogs will figure out their structure pretty quick and since the dog park is more of a neutral, shared territory, one won't have the ability to posture over others. But pack dynamics and training concerns are something to consider before ever taking your dog to a dog park. Also, check your city's regulations; some breeds may not be allowed at dog parks and other rules may exist. At the least, make sure your dog is current on vaccinations so that they will be resilient to any canine diseases they may come in contact with while interacting with other dogs. I personally don't engage either of the aforementioned techniques, as I prefer to avoid the risks and prefer to handle my dog in a much more controlled environment with fewer distractions. But know that taking your dog to doggy day care or a dog park can be beneficial in not only letting off steam, but also for socializing your pup.

Mental Exercise and Combatting Boredom

HELPFUL TIP
Bloodhounds Aren't Porch Dogs

While Blood-hounds are often portrayed as being happy to snooze on a porch all day, they need quite a bit of exercise every day. In fact, you should never rely on a Bloodhound to stay put on a porch—he should always be in a fenced yard or on a leash due to the breed's tendency to follow their nose anywhere it leads.

Physical exercise is probably the most important thing you can give to your Bloodhound. It helps tire them out and prevents behaviors caused by boredom. But mental exercise is equally important for your Bloodhound. Now, I've mentioned that hounds are stubborn, primal, and aloof animals. What I may not have emphasized as much is how smart they are too. Bloodhounds are extremely good at reading social cues and empathy. Along with their intelligence, they are also a bit neurotic and obsessive when it comes to certain things. For example, when they lock onto a scent, nothing will stop them from trying to track it down. They will constantly sniff around and smell anything new. That intelligence is what leads to a lot of their struggles, so giving them something to do with their brain is just as important as working out their body.

Toys are a good way to allow your Bloodhound to stretch their brain muscles. As Heather Pearson from Black Diamond Bloodhounds and Bracco Italianos points out, "Having a Bloodhound can be compared to having a 100 lb toddler. If they get bored, they will find something to get into. However, if you provide mental stimulation and exercise they are less likely to seek their own entertainment." Toys that allow you to hide treats inside them will provide hours of fun for your pup. It is exciting to watch them use their nose to identify where the treat is hidden inside the toy, and then come up with ways to get to it. I have a heavy rubber toy that I will put peanut butter into and will then watch my dog use his tongue and paws to get every last bit out. Not only does he get a treat out of it, but it allows him to use his instincts to accomplish a goal. Ultimately, it is working out his brain and stimulating him so he doesn't turn to other behaviors to keep himself occupied.

Finding toys that will truly stimulate your Bloodhound like this can be hard as Bloodhounds are such strong chewers. Many toys with squeakers will be destroyed within minutes and only reinforce destructive behaviors in your dog. Spend time looking for something strong that will withstand their tough jaws and also provide some sort of stimulation and reward. Keeping your hound busy in body and mind will ultimately help lead them to healthy nondestructive behaviors in your home.

Cues Bloodhound's Give When They Aren't Getting What They Need

We've established that Bloodhounds need tons of stimulation and exercise and when you see your hound sleeping at the end of a long day, you will understand why. Tiring out your dog will keep them busy and prevent them from resorting to destructive behaviors. A lack of exercise will present itself in the form of things like digging, barking, and the infamous zoomies. Zoomies are a phenomenon where your dog will all of a sudden get a large bout of energy and start running in circles and otherwise just going crazy. These outbursts of energy come from a lack of external stimulation and are episodes where spare energy is exerted quickly. They can cause your dog to run around, tearing up the yard or furniture as they jump and stride over anything in their path.

Similarly, digging and excessive barking can occur because of a build-up of energy. The dog will look for ways to get their exercise in whether you like it or not, so try to find ways to use that energy constructively, rather than letting your dog resort to their own means of getting it out. Many bad Bloodhound behaviors can be easily resolved by examining their exercise routine and making changes to it. So pay attention to your Bloodhound, and if they are doing something they were trained not to do or are being destructive, ask yourself if they are a lost cause, or really, and more likely, just bored.

CHAPTER 11
Basic Household Training

"Be patient! Bloodhounds are a stubborn breed but don't confuse that with not being smart."

Kevin Weitkamp
Black River Bloodhounds

Start Young and Remain Confident

Photo Courtesy of
Julie Shangraw

In previous chapters, we discussed Bloodhound behaviors and shared some tips and tricks for training them. This chapter will go more into training your dog and offer you insights into how and why certain training techniques work. Up until this point, we've focused on reinforcing behavior through praise and rewards, and we will dive a bit deeper into that in the following pages. Of course, if you got your dog as a puppy, you'll have plenty of time to groom and train them to become the best pup they can be. These techniques are also useful if you have an older dog as it will help you understand the psychology behind what your dog is thinking when you are teaching them.

But the main thing to remember is to stay confident. You have established yourself as the Alpha and now you must maintain that position so your hound doesn't try to take over. As your Bloodhound gets bigger, they will start to become aware of their own strength, and will challenge the social structure from time to time. Don't let them push you around, intimidate you, or tire you out. Stay confident and consistent and maintain your spot as their leader. If your Bloodhound senses any slack or leniency for their behaviors, they will muscle their way through and those minor inconveniences could turn into huge problems. So, stock up on some treats, practice that stern voice, and get ready to practice some canine psychology.

Pavlov and You – How Operant Conditioning Works

When it comes to household training, you have to understand the foundations of a few psychological principles if you wish to have success with your pup. I won't go into too much detail, as I don't want this bringing back nightmares of college lectures, but we will touch on the basic principles of conditioning.

Most people have probably heard of Pavlov and his experiments with dogs. Pavlov found that he could get a dog to salivate simply by ringing a bell through what is now known as

HELPFUL TIP
Kind Leader Versus Cruel Boss

Bloodhounds are strong-willed and need to understand that you're the boss. However, they are extremely sensitive and don't respond well to punishment. Instead, focus on rewarding your Bloodhound for desirable behaviors. He should understand that all good things, including food, come from you—and only when he behaves appropriately.

classical conditioning. To do this, Pavlov would introduce a treat so that the dogs would start salivating, and then he would ring a bell. Over time and through continuous exposure to these stimuli, the dogs would unconsciously start salivating merely at the sound of the bell. The treat would not have to even be present, as the autonomic response was conditioned so that the auditory sound of the bell would cause salivation. From this, people were able to deduce that behavior could be manipulated by the introduction of outside stimuli. This led to its implication in shaping and molding desirable behaviors through reinforcement and punishment.

The difference between classical conditioning and operant conditioning, which is what we will discuss next, is the nature of the response generated through the introduced stimuli. Classical conditioning elicits an unconscious response, whereas operant conditioning brings on a conscious and motivated decision to do something. This may all seem complicated, but the odds are you already employ aspects of operant conditioning in other parts of your life, so now we just need to focus them on training your Bloodhound.

In operant conditioning, there are a few key terms we need to establish to fully lay the groundwork for what's to come. Operant conditioning sets out to train a response based on reinforcement or punishment. Reinforcement means that we want the behavior to increase or become the norm. Punishment means we want the behavior to decrease. With both items, there is a positive way of doing things and a negative way. This is not a qualifier on how effective they are, but rather what it means

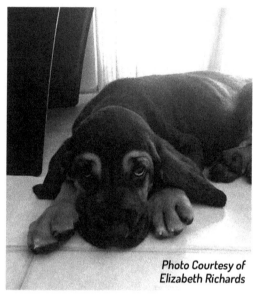

Photo Courtesy of Elizabeth Richards

is that positive conditioning adds something to the environment, and negative takes something away.

An easy way to understand this is by looking at how we teach children to do things. Let's imagine a teenager who is in school. If they come home with good grades on their report cards, parents will celebrate this and give them praise and maybe take them out for ice cream as a job well done. This is positive reinforcement. The praise and ice cream are being introduced to encourage the child to continue getting good grades. On the other hand, if the report card comes back with bad grades, the parents will potentially take away something from the child like a toy or TV. This is a negative punishment. The toy is being taken away from their environment in hopes of decreasing the behavior of getting bad grades.

Sometimes the terminology of positive and negative conditioning can be confusing because we naturally think of negative as bad and positive as good. In this sense, try to think of the words in math terms. One is adding and the other is taking away. Most commonly, we will hear the term positive reinforcement being used in encouraging behavior, but negative reinforcement and positive punishment can be used just as effectively.

An example of these would be to think about a dog that has a pinch or choke collar on. As the dog is out on a walk, they may start pulling on their lead, causing the collar to pinch or inflict pain. That is positive punishment. A stimulus, the pain, is introduced in hopes of decreasing the behavior of pulling. At the same time, when the dog relaxes and stops pulling, the pain goes away. That is an example of negative reinforcement. A stimulus, the pain, is taken away to encourage the behavior of relaxing and not pulling. More than likely, you will use a combination of these techniques when training your hound. Now that you know what they are, you can put them in your training toolbox and choose the appropriate one for different situations.

Reinforcement and Your Bloodhound's Fragile Psyche

Throughout this book, I have focused heavily on the use of positive reinforcement in training your Bloodhound. I will stick by this as being the most effective way to get your hound to behave. But don't get me wrong, it's not always going to be sunshine and rainbows, and maintaining a positive attitude is not always realistic. At times, frustration will get the best of you and punishing your dog will seem like your only remaining option. I am by no means an advocate of animal abuse, but some of the cliché punishments like rubbing their nose in their pee or swatting them with a rolled up newspaper will probably seem tempting from time to time.

While those punishments may seem perfectly acceptable and well deserved when you are at your wits' end, from my experience, they just don't have the impact you would hope. I tried everything with my hound, and potty training proved to be one of our biggest obstacles. He could hold it and demonstrated that by not using his crate as a bathroom

Photo Courtesy of Mike and Dina Whalen

Photo Courtesy of Tad and Jennifer Person

when he was locked in it at night. But once I gave him the freedom to roam about freely at night, he started lifting his leg on everything. After many mornings of stepping in puddles of pee or busting out the carpet cleaner to treat the carpets, I finally started doing some research and seeing what I was doing wrong. I would get mad at my hound for peeing on the floor. I'd put him outside and not let him come in for a while. I thought I was punishing him, when in reality, I was reinforcing his behavior. I thought I was discouraging the peeing by taking away his ability to be inside with me. But to him, I was rewarding him by letting him go outside and play and smell all the things in the outside world. Yelling at him in the morning when I found the pee didn't work either, because the behavior had already come and gone. When I was yelling, I wasn't punishing the peeing behavior, but whatever it was he was doing right then.

So again, consistency and supervision are key. Your punishments, and more importantly reinforcements, need to be timely. They need to accompany the behavior you wish to change, or else your hound will become confused and you may end up affecting a behavior you didn't mean to.

Focusing on Rewards for Good Behavior, Not Punishment for Bad Behavior

Over time and through a lot of trial and error, I realized that Bloodhounds are actually very sensitive creatures. Their disposition in this regard should play heavily in how you decide to train them. I mentioned that Bloodhounds have a fragile psyche, and that will lead them to get discouraged if your training regimen isn't consistent with their needs. Their sensitivity and constant desire to please can cause them to lose focus on what they are trying to learn if you punish them when they really just need reinforcement. For instance, if you are training your dog to track a scent or find a person that hiding, it's best to ignore their mistakes and redirect their attention than to punish them. If they are punished or scolded, they will start focusing on behavior that earns your affection back, rather than the task at hand.

When it comes down to it, Bloodhounds just want to be loved. When you punish them, they may lose track of what they are doing in a desperate attempt to win you over again. Because of this, I found it most effective to use positive reinforcement with my dog and to reward him with affection. Some dogs are food motivated and that works great in training, but you want to eventually have them obey without needing to carry a pocketful of treats around with you. When they do the right thing, be over the top and happy about it. Use an affectionate tone and pet and rub them in their favorite spot. Tell them loudly what a good dog they are.

When I first started this, it felt unnatural and fake in how over the top I was being with my dog. I'd find pee in the house, and rather than getting mad, I'd take him outside and pretend like I was lifting my leg on things in the backyard. When he'd go over and follow suit, I would boisterously tell him what a good dog he was. I'd pet him and rub his favorite spot on his chest and smile at him. I repeated this over the course of a few days, multiple times a day. By the end of it, he was going outside and lifting his leg even if he didn't have to pee, just to get my attention and get the love. Obviously, he had been positively conditioned to know that when he lifts his leg, he got attention. Over time, it took less and less reinforcement to get him to go where he was expected to. But even after the behavior is established, it's good to continue to reinforce it so that the bad behaviors don't rear their ugly head.

Photo Courtesy of
Lindsey Norman

Are Training Classes Right for You and Your Bloodhound?

Even with all the praise and punishment and treats and scolding, sometimes it's time to admit that you and your dog need help. Don't view this as a bad thing if you need to enlist the assistance of a professional dog trainer. There are a lot of options out there to help you and your dog get to a place where you can live with and trust each other completely. There are, of course, expensive puppy training classes you can enroll your hound in where they will go to a facility and be conditioned by professionals. This can be extremely useful if you don't have the time or energy to put into fully training your dog. The biggest issue I have with having someone else train your dog is that the most crucial part of your dog's training is having them obey you. You need to build up the trust and assert yourself as their leader for you to truly be in control of them and their behavior. After all, you are going to want to make sure that you have your Bloodhound in control or else you or someone you know may end up getting hurt.

That's why I recommend taking classes where you are involved with the professional trainer. Find a place where they will teach you how to train your pup, rather than some stranger doing it for you. This will build your own abilities, help get your dog's behaviors in check, and will also build the relationship and trust between you and your dog. If you haven't noticed, being confident and consistent has been a theme throughout this book. Those attributes will be undeniable in their importance of building and maintaining a happy and healthy life for you and your hound. In the end, your Bloodhound will love and respect you for teaching them to be the lovable slobber monsters they were destined to be.

CHAPTER 12
Basic Commands

"Bloodhounds are not the easiest dogs to train. They can be very hard headed. I suggest you start from the moment you get the puppy. Simple things like having them sit before a treat. Most are food motivated and will cooperate decently for treats. Be patient, consistent and POSITIVE. They may be XL dogs, but they get their feelings hurt very easily."

Heather Pearson
Black Diamond Bloodhounds & Bracco Italianos

Benefits of Proper Training

At this point, you should have a fairly firm grasp on how you're going to go about training your Bloodhound. You've learned about canine psychology and understand some of the emotional and physical needs of your dog. This is where it really all starts coming together. It's the test part of the course, if you will. Odds are, you've already been putting a lot of effort into training your dog where to go to the bathroom and how to behave, so now it's time to teach them tricks. We will go over some of the more common tricks like sit and stay, and explain why they are so much more than just ways to show off your pup's talents. Many of the commands you teach your Bloodhound will have implications in training them for larger and more complex tasks. But before we can really expect them to walk on a leash like a pro, or track down a two-day-old scent, we have to lay the foundation for those behaviors. Simple commands like sit and stay will be excellent not only in gaining control of your hound, but in getting them to focus. Believe it or not, when done right, getting your dog to follow a command can actually be used to condition another behavior. Bloodhounds love to work. They love having a purpose, so training them can actually be a good way to help them burn some of that excess energy we've talked about so much. Getting your Bloodhound to listen is a trick in itself, but with the knowledge you've been armed with up to this point, I have confidence that you're up to the task.

Like I said, basic commands are going to be the foundation for training your dog to do bigger tasks. Having a grasp on your dog's core training will make these tasks infinitely easier. For most dogs, their first trick or command will be sit. This will prove itself useful over and over again as you use it to refocus your dog and bring them back to a calm state. Over time your dog will be conditioned to know that when they sit, they have to do it calmly before getting their reward.

A good example to show how ubiquitous this command will be is to look at when you take your dog on a walk. You may cross streets, come across other dogs or people, or have a loud car come by and scare your dog. By getting them to sit, you get them to refocus from whatever the external stimulus is that has gotten them off track, and make them focus on one thing they do really well. When you come up to a street you need to cross, you're going to want to make your dog sit, and only when they can perform that task do they get to move on and continue walking. This progression will ensure that your dog is calm and that if they ever do get away from you, they will know they aren't supposed to go in the street unless invited to do so.

The importance of having a good grasp on basic commands will prove itself useful in so many situations that it should be something you put as much effort into as possible. Even if you forget everything you read in this book and only remember one thing, try to remember that training your dog basic commands will make your life infinitely easier.

Photo Courtesy of
Clive Norman

89

Finding What Motivates Your Bloodhound

HELPFUL TIP
Finding the Right Reward

Your Blood hound may or may not be food motivated enough to obey your commands for treats. Maybe he would prefer a favorite toy, praise, or the chance to smell something new as a reward for obeying you. Figure out what works best for your Bloodhound and stick with it.

As you were reading above, you probably thought to yourself that training a dog is no big deal and that it can't be that hard to make a Bloodhound sit. But getting a Bloodhound to do anything besides drooling and being a goofball is insanely difficult. I'll say it again, Bloodhounds are extremely stubborn. They will do what they want to do and follow their nose above all else. If your attempts at training them interfere with their plans, you will most likely be ignored and told loudly through their baying that you are in the wrong.

With that being said, there is a way to tame the wild beast. The best way to get a Bloodhound to pay attention is to find what motivates them. The tried and true fallback is usually treats or food. Most Bloodhounds will be food motivated and the use of small treats can be a great way to get your dog to listen to you. Brenda Olive from Hickory Ridge Kennel notes that "a hungry Bloodhound will train easier than a full one if using food as a reward. Always use positive reinforcement."

Using treats is probably the most common way of training basic commands. With mine, for instance, if I give him a treat, he will hold it in his mouth for a second and then spit it out, in anticipation of another one. Only when I walk away and stop paying attention will he take the time to actually eat what he was given. This is more of a recent behavior and as a puppy I used a lot of treats to motivate him. The problem with it was that buying dog treats all the time quickly got expensive and I resorted to finding other items that were in the house. To this day, if anyone pulls one of those mozzarella string cheeses out of my fridge, my hound immediately goes to his crate and waits for it. That's because I would reward and lure him into his crate with string cheese when he was younger, and he has been conditioned to think that when string cheese comes out, it's time to go to the crate.

While the string cheese is a good example of food being used as a motivator, it's usually not my go-to training aid. I recommend using praise and affection as reinforcement whenever possible. This way you can still get your dog to behave when you are away from home or may have forgotten their treats. Each dog will react differently based on their personality and needs, so pay attention to what works for your dog in particular and you will have success in motivating them to do what you want them to do.

A Bloodhound's Desire to Work

Photo Courtesy of Kathryn Robinson

One thing you should definitely have picked up on by now is that a tired Bloodhound is a happy Bloodhound. They have tons of energy and they love to work. So don't feel bad that you are putting them through a strict training regimen. Your Bloodhound will thank you for taking the time and effort to train them and to use their excess energy in a constructive way. I've mentioned before that I use a correction collar for getting my dog's attention. At first I was mortified and felt like a bad owner putting on the collar. But even with my reservations, I had seen how quickly the vibrate function and sound got his attention, so decided to give it a go. I used it primarily for training him to walk, but wish I had found it sooner to train him basic commands. The thing is, as I used it more, he began to associate the collar with work time. As soon as he saw it, he would sit down and await me putting on the collar. To my amazement, he actually liked the time with the collar, because when he saw it, he knew it meant exercise and work, and ultimately attention and treats. To this day I still use it. Not out of necessity because he's pretty well-behaved, but because it's part of the routine. And, as we've established, routines and proper expectations make your endeavors with your Bloodhound all the more pleasant.

*Photo Courtesy of
Kendall Alguire*

Basic Commands and How to Teach Them

So we've talked about how to get your dog to pay attention, how to reward them, and how to identify their unique motivational characteristics. Now comes the time to actually teach them their first commands. I like to pair my commands with a hand gesture. That way I can get the dog's attention and give him the serious glare that most parents do so well, and get him to obey with just a hand signal. These hand signals may be different for everyone and it really doesn't matter what they are. But the main thing you want to do is pair the verbal command with a hand signal so you can condition the desired response to both stimuli.

First off, let's get your dog to learn the most basic and useful command of sitting. Have your treats or reward ready and get your dog in an area free of distractions. Start by standing in front of them and telling them to sit. I snap my fingers and point at the ground for this one. As a puppy, your dog will have no idea what this means and will need some assistance. Gently push on their rear end to get them in a sitting position and immediately reward them. Even if they stand back up, every time you push them into the sitting position, reward them right away. It will take some time for them to get the hang of what they are supposed to do, so do it over and over again. Eventually, your dog will start to get the hang of what you are trying to do and may start squatting rather than fully sitting. This is at least an attempt and should be rewarded.

Over time you want to be more and more strict as to what they need to do to get the treat. At first, sitting with your assistance or a gentle nudge is fully acceptable as we are just introducing the desired behavior. Then squatting will be the only way they can achieve the treat. After some time of them squatting, start being more strict. Tell them no, repeat the command, and push their bottom down all the way again to get them in the sitting position. What this is doing is telling the dog that they were on the right track, but must complete the action fully to get the reward. Once they start sitting on their own, you can also pat yourself on the back and give yourself a treat. You have taught a trick to one of the most stubborn creatures known to man. Congratulations.

Getting your hound to sit is the cornerstone of other tricks and commands to come. The other commands you will treat your Bloodhound will usually start with sitting, so make sure to spend the time reinforcing it, before moving on to these next commands.

Getting your dog to stay is the next crucial task you want to put in front of your hound. Once they are sitting, you want them to stay sitting or stay where you want them. It's not uncommon for your dog to mas-

*Photo Courtesy of
Lillian Brock*

ter sit, and then do it for a fraction of a second before getting a treat. Getting them to stay will exert that control and dominance over them and ultimately get them to listen to you more by building trust. Your dog will learn through staying put that you follow through with the reward, but on your terms. They don't just simply have to do an action to get the treat, but must do it to your satisfaction.

To train stay, I use an open hand or halt signal paired with the command. Try getting your dog to sit, then hold up your hand with your palm toward them, and start taking steps backward away from them. As your dog gets up to follow you, make them start over. Get them to sit, and begin the process again. Start small. As you take just a few steps and your dog stays put, give them a treat. Increase the distance required each time and demand more from your hound. The goal here is to be able to back up or walk out of their view with them staying put in the place you left them. This is a good test in building the bond and trust between you and your dog as they must implicitly believe you are coming back to reward them. The key is that each time they get up and try to start getting closer, quickly correct them and start over. You need to condition the idea that they must sit in place until you beckon them to come over. Again, you want to start small with this and celebrate small victories. Over time, increase your distance and expectations of your hound, and challenge them to stay focused on the reward.

The last main command we will talk about is lying down. This is the final step in exerting your dominance over your dog by making them literally bow down to you. By teach them to lie down, you are making them willingly submissive to you. Lying down is a good command for training your dog when it's okay to bother you or approach or when they should leave you alone.

I use lie down a lot during dinner time. Since a Bloodhound is so big, they will sit next to the table, prop their head up on the side of it, and stare at you and your food as rivers of drool encroach closer and closer to your mashed potatoes. By telling them to lie down, they are being told they are not physically on the same level as you and that they must submit and complete that trick before getting any food. Be ready to reward them after dinner with a treat if they successfully leave you alone.

To help your dog to learn to lie down, use the signal of pointing at the ground. Start them off by getting them to sit, and then taking their treat and holding it in your hand on the ground in front of them. You may have to pull their front legs out from under them to help them get in the position a few times. Get them into a prone state, and then immediately reward them. Pair lying down with staying so that your dog knows that when they lie down, they are to do it until you tell them otherwise.

Photo Courtesy of Vicky Pittsley

Use confidence and don't get frustrated. You will notice when your dog is confused or needs to be refocused because they will start trying to do any trick they know to get the treat. Take a step back, get them to sit, and then start getting them to lie down again. Don't lose focus on your goal, and reinforce any small wins with treats and love. By teaching your dog these foundational commands, you will be well on your way to having a strong dog that is submissive to you as their leader.

You will want to teach your dog other commands like shake or roll over, but those are more for show. They don't serve a purpose for further training outside of having them listen to you. You're going to want to do your best to find a way to teach your dog to drop things that they pick up in their mouths too. My best recommendation to teach this is to get your dog's attention by telling them to sit and stay, and then telling them to "drop it" or "leave it." Now, odds are that your Bloodhound will disregard this command because they are so stubborn. But I find that distracting them with a treat they enjoy can yield some results in getting them to drop whatever is in their mouth. Bloodhounds have extremely strong jaws, and when they get something they aren't supposed to have, they will lock down and run away to chew and gnaw on whatever it is. I've spent a lot of time chasing my hound in circles as he runs away from me with a paper towel in his mouth. Once I catch him, I've found the only way to get it away is to reach into his slobber hole and fish it out with my fingers or entice him with a different treat. It's almost as if all training and commands go out the window as he tries his hardest to chew whatever the item is and swallow it before I can even get close. All joking aside, this is a situation where your other training comes in, as you can command them to sit, get them to focus, and remind them who's boss. Catching a Bloodhound who is up to no good is a task within itself, so use the tools in your arsenal to get them to listen and assert your dominance.

CHAPTER 13:
Advanced Training – Using Your Bloodhound's Nose

"Bloodhounds are famous for their noses. Their nose can smell things we can't imagine. This ability to smell can make for a wonderful working dog, or a wonderful pet. Many bloodhounds have a lot of drive. They are athletic, and busy following their keen sense of smell."

__Brenda Olive__
Hickory Ridge Kennel

An Introduction in "Man Trailing"

When someone hears the term "Bloodhound," it usually invokes thoughts of a dog with their nose to the ground tracking something. Their nose is their most powerful feature, and has been used for centuries to track down animals and people. Early in their history, they were used primarily as hunting dogs to track down deer and boars. As time went on, their exceptional nose was used to find people. Whether tracking escaped convicts or lost hikers, Bloodhounds have proven their worth in following a scent time and time again. It's because of this exceptional history that Bloodhounds are employed by law enforcement and search and rescue teams across the world.

The art of tracking down a person through a primary scent is known in many circles as "man-trailing." There are many techniques to condition your dog to be a world-class tracker, and training them can be a life-long endeavor. Their noses can always be more refined and they can practice being more focused as time goes on. Kevin Weitkamp from Black River Bloodhounds advises to "...let them use their nose. Their purpose in life is their nose, they have to utilize it."

So, if this is the route you want to go with your hound, it's best to start young so you can teach them to follow the scent you need them to, rather than allowing them the freedom to sniff out what's interesting to them. Man-trailing and tracking is such an in-depth and lengthy pro-

Photo Courtesy of
Alicia Cheshire

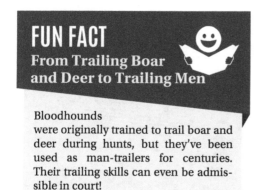

FUN FACT

From Trailing Boar and Deer to Trailing Men

Bloodhounds were originally trained to trail boar and deer during hunts, but they've been used as man-trailers for centuries. Their trailing skills can even be admissible in court!

cess that I could fill a whole book with techniques and tips for accomplishing it. In fact, there are books and groups that exist that will aid in teaching this amazing skill. This chapter will be an introductory guide into tracking. It is in no way a comprehensive guide and if you want to turn your dog into a certified tracking animal, I encourage you to seek those groups out for all the support and education you need. What you will find in this chapter is a more novice approach to tracking so that anyone, regardless of desired outcome, can enjoy their Bloodhound's nose and experience how strong they are.

Refining Your Dog's Nose and Getting Them to Focus

When you get your hound, you will undoubtedly notice them sniffing around and using their nose constantly. They have a distinctive pose when they are tracking something. Their heads will be down to the ground, and their tail will stand up with a slight curve toward their heads. It is an iconic look and one that will make you beam with pride that you have such an impressive dog. Their natural nature is to smell things and follow scents. The real trick is getting them to follow the scents that you want them to follow. Because they are so stubborn and have so much energy, it is easy for them to become distracted and follow whatever thing grabs their attention. We touched on this before when talking about keeping your dog on a leash. They will follow any scent that intrigues them, and they will follow it even amidst your redirections and pleads not to.

This is why it's important to refine your hound's nose through conditioning. What you want to do is get your dog to not necessarily ignore other distracting scents, but to assign a priority to which ones will garner the biggest reward of finding. In the past, hunters always saved a special reward from whatever animal it was that the hound was trailing. This could be a piece of the hide or antlers of a deer. It was something so good, the hound would pass up on other competing scents to zero in on the track that got them that reward.

Obviously, if the hound is tracking a person, we won't be able to reward them with something to eat when they succeed, but we can encourage them with love and praise or even a special toy reserved only for when they accomplish their job. You'll see this a lot of times in law enforcement, where a dog successfully tracks down a criminal and rather than biting away on the assailant, they get a toy. This redirects the hound and lets them know they completed their task. The toy must be something special and not something that is used for other training. It has to have a special meaning and be perceived as the ultimate reward for tracking down their target. So again, find something special that motivates your individual dog, and use that to your advantage.

To start training your dog to track, you can employ some exercises in your home to get them thinking about what they need to do. Start with small treats or toys they like and make a trail by dragging that item across the floor. Try to get your dog out of view so they can't watch what you're doing and run the item along the floor in circles, over furniture and in a generally haphazard pattern. You will be amazed as your dog comes into the room and starts following the scent. You will watch as they get into their iconic pose and start sniffing away, going in circles, over furniture, and essentially following every step that item took to get it to its final resting spot. If your hound gets distracted and starts going off the rails, redirect them. Get their attention and point back to one of the spots the item they are tracking touched and get them to refocus on it. Soon enough, they will discover the item and that's when it's time for

Photo Courtesy of
Sue Daniel

Photo Courtesy of Michelle Mantilla

the reward. Reinforce the behavior with love and giving them the treat they just tracked down. As you practice this, they will be able to do it faster and more accurately over time.

Once they have it down in your home, take them outside and expand the search area. Keep them on a leash so you can aid them in redirecting focus if they start to stray. Try not to punish your dog for losing the trail, as this can add a negative connotation to the job they are doing and ultimately discourage them. If they get off scent, refocus them to the last point they had the trail and give them some praise. Tracking is a constant exercise in reinforcement until they reach their ultimate goal of finding the source of their trail.

In hunting, a lot of people will use blood from an animal because blood has such a unique scent and invokes an almost primal desire in your Bloodhound. Many people who teach this method will use blood obtained from a fresh animal they hunted or from their local butcher. Blood also has such a unique smell that it will often stand out more than just fur or something that brushed along the ground. Also, most animals aren't always bleeding when they are running around in the wild, so by training your dog to follow a blood scent, they will be able to better identify what they are trying to track rather than getting confused by all the other contact scents they may come across. Whether you are training for hunting or man-trailing, refining your dog's nose and getting them to assign priority to scents will be crucial in getting them to achieve their ultimate goal.

Search and Rescue

Their ability to track hurt or injured animals and people is why Bloodhounds are commonly used for search and rescue. Many times, people who wander into the wild and get lost end up getting hurt and require a crew to come in and help them get out. Tracking a blood scent is probably the easiest way for a hound to track someone down, but what if there isn't blood? Many search

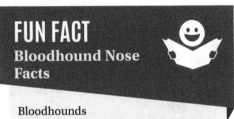

FUN FACT
Bloodhound Nose Facts

Bloodhounds have the most scent receptors of any dog breed—around 250-300 million! They can follow a scent trail that was left more than a week previously, and they can follow a scent trail for more than 130 miles.

and rescue teams will ask for an item that the target has come in contact with. This could be an article of clothing or the interior of a vehicle. What they are looking for is anything that has a strong enough and easily identifiable scent that the hound can lock onto and focus on amongst all the other smells the world.

Some police departments and rescue groups will provide families with scent kits. These are kits that will have an item a person can wear or sleep with that will get their scent on it. These kits can then be saved for later so that if the need for them ever arises, an item with a primary scent is readily available for a hound to track. I trained my dog to do this by sleeping with a stuffed animal for about a week. I then took my wife out to the wilderness and I took off hiking while they waited back at the trailhead in the car. As I was walking, I made a point to rub up on bushes and drag my feet a bit. I wandered on and off the trail so that my dog could lock on my scent and disregard any competing scents. After I had hiked about a mile, my wife introduced the stuffed animal to our dog. He sniffed it, played with it a bit, and locked onto the scent. She then directed him to the trail I had taken off on, and to her amazement, he started tracking me. He followed my line as I wandered on and off the trail and would stop at bushes I had rubbed upon to solidify his grasp on the scent. Within an hour, my hound led my wife to the tree I was sitting under in a little arroyo about a hundred yards off the trail. Now, I had never planned on making my dog a search and rescue dog and didn't invest a lot of training into it as he was more intended to be a family pet. But his innate sense of smell and desire to track led him to me with a very basic training of how to refine and follow his nose.

How to Read Your Dog's Cues

When you are out on the trail or in your backyard teaching your dog to track, keep an eye on their body behavior and cues. They will often look to you as their leader if they get confused or need direction. Since you have established yourself as their pack leader, they may look to you for help when they are struggling to find their trail. It's important to keep an eye on them and be able to read your dog so that they don't get too far off track.

You will notice they are starting to fade when their tail drops from the upright position, or when they start walking with their head up from the ground. Take it slow and make a mental note of the last spot they were able to catch the scent they are trailing. If they get distracted, get them to sit and start paying attention to your command, and take them back to the last area they were displaying the signs of tracking. Reinforce and encourage them by giving them so love and appreciation, telling them how good they are doing. Allow them to stop and have a drink of water. They are built for endurance but will start frothing at the mouth if they are working too hard. Allow them to take a break and don't rush them. If they get too frantic, they will begin to lose focus. You want your hound to be calm and determined to find their target, not curling up to take a snooze in the sun. Just pay attention to them and what their body language tells you, so you can form a team in tracking down whatever you are looking for.

Photo Courtesy of Kathryn Robinson

Fun Facts About Following Tracks

Having a Bloodhound comes with a lot of joys and frustrations, but watching them track a scent will undoubtedly fill you with pride and admiration. After all, their nose is their most iconic feature and it's important to harness that trait and let them use it to its fullest extent. Their nose is so strong and reliable, it can be introduced in court as evidence. They are the only animal that can be said to have this ability. Even other drug- or bomb-sniffing dogs can't claim this achievement. Other dogs can signal their handlers to an area that needs to be searched, but it's ultimately the handler whose testimony would be used in court. A Bloodhound's ability to track can stand on its own. In fact, their nose is so strong, it can find and track a trail that is almost two weeks old. Everything about their appearance is designed to capture and track an individual scent. And they have so many scent receptors that they can easily distinguish minor nuances between competing smells. All these factors help the Bloodhound stand out through the ages as the most reliable and effective scent hound in existence.

CHAPTER 14
Identifying and Correcting Bad Behavior

"The most common bad behavior I hear about is Resource Guarding. Get a professional trainer to help you, but start early. Don't give up on the dog when it starts displaying this behavior; just help them work through it. Food aggression: be present when you feed them right from the beginning with your puppy. And have your hand in their food, have the kids do the same."

Deborah Thompson
Cyclone Ridge Kennels

Is It Bad Behavior or Inconvenient Behavior

Owning a Bloodhound is kind of a mixed bag. On one hand, you will revel in and be amazed by their innate senses and abilities when it comes to tracking. On the other, you will be truly dumbfounded by their aloof and sometimes excruciatingly frustrating behavior. Bloodhounds have certain behaviors caused by their stubbornness that will have you pulling your hair out. Some of these behaviors could include their loud baying at seemingly mundane things, their complete disregard for personal space, or their predisposition to standing on counters and tables. Odds are that if you own a Bloodhound, you've already experienced some of these behaviors and are at a loss for how to overcome them.

I hate being the bearer of bad news, but some of these behaviors just come with the territory. Bloodhounds aren't a good dog to have if you live in an apartment or require a pristine home. Bloodhounds are dirty animals. Some of them drool constantly, their ears drag in the dirt, water pours out of their mouth and across the floor when they drink. These are things that should be expected and not something you hope to train your dog not to do. I wish, above all else, that my dog wouldn't turn on his mouth sprinklers when a guest arrives in my home. Without fail, he does what I call the Bloodhound handshake. He walks right up to whoever entered the home and wants to greet them by smelling their crotch. Pair that with the drool coming out of his mouth due to excitement and many guests have left needing a wardrobe change.

Photo Courtesy of
Terri Senecal

Obviously I can put my dog in the backyard or separate them from guests, but sometimes I want to let him be free. I don't ever expect to change this behavior as it is something that he does. It's a quirk or a personality trait and as hard as I may try, he simply won't stop doing it. So, if you can't beat them join them. It's for this reason that I have an apron hanging by my door so that guests can put it on and enjoy their visit without having to worry about immediately doing a load of laundry due to drool stains when they get home.

Much like the aforementioned drooling episodes, Bloodhounds will have many behaviors that are just part of the breed. When you're trying to train your Bloodhound, it's important to determine if the unwanted behavior is actually bad, or just inconvenient. Many of the inconvenient behaviors Bloodhounds exhibit aren't untrainable. You simply will not be able to get a Bloodhound to stop drooling, or stop baying when they see something that scares them. You can try your hardest to get a Bloodhound to know that they are not, in fact, lap dogs, but you will most likely be wasting time and energy.

Try to identify the traits of your dog that can actually be corrected and aren't part of their inherent nature. For example, counter surfing is a behavior you can try to train out of them. Use a correction collar or some other punishment to get them to get down if you find them up on a table. Since this behavior is usually just done as social posturing, you can attempt to get them to learn that if they do it, they will be punished. If your dog is digging holes in the backyard, use some techniques to get them to stop. These behaviors are inconvenient and destructive and with good training and attention can be eradicated. But things like drooling and barking are just part of owning a Bloodhound and you should embrace them and wear your drool-soaked clothes as a badge of honor.

Outward Behaviors and Finding the Root Cause

Although it may be hard to hear, sometimes our Bloodhound's actions are directly caused by things we do as owners. It may not necessarily be the Bloodhound's behavior that needs to change, but our own. The outward behaviors that your dog exhibits are a reflection of their environment and upbringing. I'm sure you've heard of nature vs. nurture, and honestly, it's a pretty even split between the two. Sure, your dog's natural characteristics will play a role in how they act. But how we treat them and address their needs will also play a huge role in their outward expressions of behavior.

Changes in the Environment/Household

Before grabbing the correction collar or raising your voice at your hound, take a step back and see if something you're doing is causing the behavior. If your dog is digging in the backyard, odds are that they are bored or have excess energy, so try to take them out on more walks. If they are being aggressive with food, make sure they are on a proper diet and eat in a safe place where they don't feel challenged for their resources. If your dog starts peeing in the home after successful potty training, try to ask yourself "What changed?" Many times, simply trying to identify external stressors and changes in your dog's environment or routine can reveal the root cause of many bad behaviors.

For example, my dog started peeing in the house after I thought I had him housebroken completely. I couldn't understand why he had all of sudden lost his mind and started lifting his leg all around my house. The behavior was so unnatural, that I began to think there may be an underlying medical cause for it. Maybe he had a kidney infection or an issue with his bladder. I made an appointment with the vet, and after repainting the walls of their office with his drool, he came back with a clean bill of health. The vet's only recommendation was to really contemplate what had changed to cause him to begin peeing in the house. I made sure I wasn't using any new cleaning products and that the cats hadn't peed or puked on any of the places he was marking.

It was about this same time that I found out my wife was pregnant. It all started coming together when I noticed my dog being more standoffish with her. He was pushing limits, not listening to commands, and in general, his whole demeanor had changed toward her. I slowly started putting it together that the change in behavior was caused by her change in hormones and smell, which his amazing nose had picked up before I even knew we were expecting.

This was a moment of enlightenment for me. I saw just how much subtle changes in my dog's environment could change his behavior. I went out, got a new toy, had my wife sleep with it and get her new scent all over it, and then had her give it to him. I had her spend extra time feeding him and getting him to listen to her.

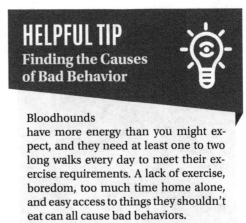

HELPFUL TIP

Finding the Causes of Bad Behavior

Bloodhounds have more energy than you might expect, and they need at least one to two long walks every day to meet their exercise requirements. A lack of exercise, boredom, too much time home alone, and easy access to things they shouldn't eat can all cause bad behaviors.

Essentially we had to treat her as a new person coming into the pack. She reasserted her place in the pack with her new smell, and within a few days, our Bloodhound was back to being the goofy and reasonably well behaved dog we had trained him to be.

So when your dog starts behaving badly, ask yourself what has changed. Take a look around your environment for any causes that could be making your dog act out. Whatever you do, don't give up hope and think your hound is just a bad dog. Most likely, they are trying to tell you in their own way that something changed and is distressing them.

Consistency in Correction

Throughout your dog's lifetime, they will need reinforcement and training on an ongoing basis. They will constantly push their luck and if they get away with something they aren't supposed to do, will continue to see how far they can push it. Stay vigilant. Your dog will thrive on consistency and routine.

Being the big dogs that they are, you will need to constantly reinforce your place as pack leader as their nature will tell them they should challenge you. Many people will shy away if their Bloodhound starts showing aggression and rightfully so. I am constantly in awe of how I have brought an animal that could easily overpower and hurt me into my home. It makes sense that people shy away from their dog when they show aggression so as not to get hurt.

Photo Courtesy of Mike and Dina Whalen

I'm not saying to necessarily challenge them or put yourself in harm's way, but try to figure out why they are all of a sudden being aggressive. A lot of times, they are trying to gain a rank in the pack. If when you try to correct them, they growl and you back away scared, they have now been conditioned that all they have to do is be aggressive and they will get what they want. Be stern and consistent, correct this behavior immediately by introducing a punishment. Stop the behavior and regain control by asserting yourself as the one in control. Show them that the behavior won't be accepted and that they need to submit to you.

Don't let bad behavior take hold, because you will have to start your training regimen over and begin to rebuild all the trust you have worked so hard to attain. Always remember that you and your family members are higher in the pack than your dog, and that you are in control of the situation. Be consistent and direct with your corrections so as not to allow bad behaviors to gain traction and take over your home.

When to Get Help

My ultimate goal throughout this journey is to empower you as a Bloodhound owner. Know that you are strong and confident and can easily tame your dog and make them into the lovable creatures they so desperately want to be. But also know when it's time to ask for help. If behaviors surface that you simply cannot stand for or control, reach out to the professionals.

I firmly believe that there is no such thing as a bad dog, just bad situations. If your dog has brought light into your life and showed you how loyal and kind they can be, don't give up on them. With Bloodhounds especially, they will make you want to pull your hair out and call it quits at times. But the work you put into training them will reward you with an unforgettable experience you will cherish for your entire life.

Too many times, when Bloodhounds start exhibiting bad or inconvenient behavior, their owners drop them off at the closest humane society or Bloodhound rescue. Honestly, your dog deserves better. You are the one constant in their lives and they have tirelessly lived to please you. Don't lose sight of that. Before getting to your wits' end and calling it quits, do everything possible to find a way to continue living with your Bloodhound. You owe it to them for their constant and undeniable devotion they have to you. Even if they don't always show it, you are their rock, and your love and adoration is their only possession in this world. If you are scared or frustrated beyond belief, ask for help before the idea of getting rid of them even creeps into your mind. Find a local trainer. Search out groups on social media. Find someone to support you in your journey and reaffirm what you know in your heart: Your Bloodhound only wants to love and be loved by you.

The 3 B's – Bad Bloodhound Behaviors

Throughout your Bloodhound's life, you will witness things that they do which will make you laugh, cry, yell, and stare at in wonder. In my house, I've deemed these as the 3 B's. The 3 B's change all the time and I'm sure you will come up with some of your own. The last 2 B's are always the same, it's just the first word that changes. You will have bad Bloodhound behavior, bewildering Bloodhound behavior, boisterous Bloodhound behavior, and even belligerent Bloodhound behavior. These dogs have such unique personalities that owning one will grant you an insight into how truly rewarding having one can be. Don't let the bad or bewildering behavior get to you. Your dog means well and at its core just wants to be a good dog. Take a step back and wonder what is causing your dog's behavior so you can better combat it and understand what they need to be happy and healthy. A tired Bloodhound is a happy Bloodhound, so spend the time working with them to reach their full potential and secure their place in your heart forever.

CHAPTER 15

Vacation – To Take Your Bloodhound or Leave Them at Home

"Bloodhounds make great travel companions if you are able to bring them along. It is a rare bloodhound that doesn't like to go and smell. They rarely get carsick, as they are not generally an anxious dog."

Brenda Olive
Hickory Ridge Kennel

Car Rides – Safety from Beginning to End

Photo Courtesy of Chelsea Amann

You've put all this time and energy into training your Bloodhound, so now it's time to take a much needed break and vacation. But what do you do with them while you're gone? Whether you're going to a faraway place, or just around the corner, you have to make a decision of what to do with your dog while you are traveling. Some excursions may allow you to bring your dog along. I have dreams of taking my Bloodhound to the beach one day, but the logistics of getting him there can seem quite daunting. Any time you go on a trip, you have to think about what you're going to do with your dog. Many options are out there, from taking them with you, to hiring a pet sitter, to boarding them at a facility. Each option comes with its own benefits and drawbacks, and

Photo Courtesy of
Amanda Riddles

Photo Courtesy of Bradley Walkup

hopefully this chapter will help inform you of what to consider when you start planning that much needed vacation.

Whether you are planning on going out of town or not, one thing you will need to figure out is how to ready your dog for rides in the car. One of the funniest things I have ever witnessed is my Bloodhound hanging out of the window with all of his flap and folds flailing in the wind. I watch as his slobber bombs fly like missiles at the cars who unluckily find themselves driving behind me.

While there is nothing like seeing the pure joy on your dog's face as they smell all the smells rushing by their nose, their safety is of utmost importance when riding in your car. There are a lot of options and devices out there that will keep you dog safe in the unfortunate case that there is an accident. Some of these devices will be helpful in making sure your dog stays in the vehicle while they are on their rides too.

Just like when they are out on walks, your hound can catch a scent and want to follow it, even if that means jumping out of a moving vehicle. One way to combat this is to get a divider for your car. If you drive an SUV or something with a large cargo area, you can get cages that will put up a divider between the passenger area and the cargo area. These will keep your dog in the back and keep you from being distracted by your dog crawling over. These are great for long trips as they give the dog a space much like their crate where they can relax, lay down and enjoy the ride.

If your car doesn't have an area like this, you can also get harnesses or tethers that will keep your dog in the backseat. These are beneficial because, again, they will keep the dog from climbing up into the front with you and causing any sort of distractions. Also, these harnesses will help restrain your dog in the event of an accident. Many dogs are killed because they are left unrestrained in a car accident and have nothing securing them. Do your dog a favor and get something that will help keep them safe when they are riding in your car. Seat belts and restraints don't only save human lives, but can save the lives of our canine companions as well.

A Home Away From Home – Making Your Dog Feel Safe on Planes and in Hotels

Driving isn't always going to be an option for many of the trips you take and you may find yourself having to prepare your dog for flying on an airplane and staying in a hotel. Being that these are going to be new experiences for your dog in new environments, your goal is to make them as comfortable as you can.

Photo Courtesy of Alyssa Snyder

Try to make the trip as familiar to them as possible. Again, Bloodhounds love a routine, so start off by getting a travel crate that you can introduce them to before going on your trip. Fill that crate with familiar blankets or toys and encourage them to spend time in there. What you're going for is to get your hound familiar with the crate so that they feel comfortable and as stress free as possible. The travel is going to be somewhat traumatic for them no matter what due to all the new sounds and smells, but you can do your best to prep them for the trip while still at home in a safe setting.

Before your trip, put the travel crate in your vehicle and have your dog get in it. This may be distressing at first as they will be used to riding in the car with a little more freedom. But as you practice, they will begin to learn that they are safe in the crate and even though they experience all the new stimuli, they come out the other side safe and secure.

This same theory applies if you have to stay at a hotel along your travels. If you have conditioned your dog to feel safe in their crate, they will have a place they can go where they can relax and feel at home. Make sure you call the hotel ahead of time and find out if they are dog-friendly and if they have any restrictions on what pets are allowed. You don't want to rack up any additional fees because of damage your hound caused to the hotel room, so combat that by trying to make the hotel feel like home. Bring some toys and treats so your dog can stay occupied. You will have to be extra vigilant in reading their cues as your hound may be confused as to how to signal they need to go the bathroom.

Whatever the case, try to make your dog familiar with the environment by bringing a piece of home with you. If your dog gets stressed out or distraught, they may resort to destructive behaviors like chewing. This will be especially true if you want to leave your dog in the hotel room while you are gone. Think of how much supervision it took to teach them not to destroy things in your own home and try to be mindful of that to avoid any damage fees. Make their crate a home away from home or a portable safe space. That way you can travel with your dog and create an enjoyable experience for both you and your Bloodhound.

Kennels vs. Dog Sitters and Services

HELPFUL TIP
Hotel Rules

Each year, it seems like more hotels are allowing dogs to stay in rooms with their owners. However, many hotels have size or breed restrictions. Even if their website claims they are dog-friendly, always call the hotel ahead of time to make sure your Bloodhound will be welcome.

More often than not, occasions will arise where you simply cannot take your hound with you when you travel and you have to make the decision of what to do with them. You can either call up a friend or a professional pet sitter and leave them at home, or take them to a boarding facility. Both have pros and cons, and you should consider what you think will make the dog most comfortable. If your dog is highly socialized and used to being around other dogs, than a boarding facility may be a great option. But if they are used to just being at home around your family, they may feel safer staying put. After all, with you being gone, your hound is going to be a little bit stressed out, so having a bit of familiarity may be a good thing. But teaching someone all your rules and inviting a relative stranger into your home may have its own challenges. What it comes down to is doing what makes you feel comfortable and will have as little impact on your dog's routine as possible.

If you go the route of finding a kennel to board them at, the first thing to do is make sure your dog is caught up on their shots. Communal boarding facilities pose the inherent risk of exposing your dog to canine diseases like Bordetella. The preventative care for Bordetella is not always required, so make sure you talk to your vet and ensure your dog is vaccinated against it. Now that you know your dog will be safe health wise, make the facility aware of any concerns you have about your dog. Make sure they are familiar with the breed and are aware of any dietary restrictions you have placed on your dog. You want the boarding facility to feel like a home away from home and be as seamless of a transition as possible. Things like feeding times, exercise routines, and other regimens will be crucial in maintaining your dog's feelings of safety and security while you are away.

If you decide to leave your dog at home and bring in a pet sitter, make sure you invite the person over to meet your dog first. Don't give a coworker a key to your home and leave them to fend for themselves. Invite them over, let them have a safe introduction with your Bloodhound, and explain any routines or requests you have for them. Try to go into as much detail about your routine as possible. After all, no one's going to know what keeps your Bloodhound in control more than you, and the last thing you want is to come home to a war zone.

When I introduce someone to my Bloodhound, I make sure to keep him calm, let him smell the other person, and give him commands while that person is present. By making him sit and do basic commands, I'm instilling in him that this person is a part of the pack and that their presence doesn't mean he can throw his training out the window. Walk the sitter through your routine of how much to feed them and how often, tell them about some of your dog's quirks, and set proper expectations of your dog's energy level. If the person is going to be taking your dog on walks, make sure you reiterate how Bloodhounds are strong pullers and will follow their nose. Basically, you want to give them a crash course on what having a Bloodhound is like. You want the person who is coming into your home to be able to seamlessly take over as Alpha while you are gone.

I recommend also writing out a list of tasks or reminders for your pet sitter. This way they have something to refer to in case they got distracted when meeting your pup for the first time. Many pet-sitting services will have the individual send pictures of your dog every day, which can help put your mind at ease. Try to keep your dog on as normal of a routine as possible because they will know that you are gone and as we've learned, changes in environment can bring out the 3 B's. So, in the end, your ultimate goal is to make your dog feel safe and secure so you can enjoy your trip and come home to an intact household and a happy hound.

CHAPTER 16
Nutrition

"Bloodhounds can be extremely protective over their food. The only thing I can recommend to do is to keep other pets and children separate from the dog while eating."

Kim Dillon
Sandstone Kennels

Why a Good Diet is Important

Having a Bloodhound comes with a lot of special considerations you must take into account to support a healthy lifestyle. We've already gone over exercise and psychological needs, and nutrition is of equal importance. After all, your Bloodhound's growth and energy will depend heavily on what you feed them. Being that Bloodhounds are large dogs, they tend to eat a lot. So choosing a dog food that's right for your dog and doesn't empty your pockets can seem like a difficult task.

There are hundreds of brands of dog food on the market and thousands of articles about what food is the "right" one for your hound. It seems like for every brand or style of dog food, there are ten people who will debate why it's the best or worst. Nowadays, navigating the playing field of competing dog foods to find one that is good for your dog and also promotes and supports their growth as a large breed is becoming increasingly difficult. Of course, the best way to find what your dog needs is to talk to your vet. They will have an understanding of exactly what your specific dog needs, and their experience with other animals of the same breed will be able to guide you in the right direction. I can only offer you what I've found through my own personal research and experience, and encourage you to seek out information about what you think is best.

This chapter will lay out some of the groundwork and fundamental principles in what Bloodhounds need at different stages of life when it comes to food. One of the best pieces of advice I can give when it comes to choosing a food is to pay attention to your dog. They will give you clues if they need something different. Find a good-quality food that is within your budget and try it out. For me, I could tell which foods didn't agree with my dog because he'd become extremely gassy on some, while with others he didn't. So try different foods and see how they react. As with all things Bloodhound, supervision is key. The ultimate goal is to give your dog what they need to grow and thrive without being too stinky and making your house smell like a fart factory.

Recommended Foods for Bloodhounds

To even begin to contemplate what kind of food you want to get your Bloodhound, it's important to know some of the fundamentals of canine nutrition. People may think of dogs as complete carnivores, meaning they only need a diet meat to survive. And while that may be partially true for wild dogs, domesticated dogs have come to be more like their human owners in that they are actually omnivores. They require nutrition from both meat and plant products to really have a balanced diet. For this reason, you will see many foods that boast a combination of vegetables and meats combined in their kibble. Plant products like sweet potatoes, sweet peas, and corn are some of the most common vegetables used to create a balanced diet for your dog.

Different types of meat will also be paired with those vegetables and deciding which one is best for your dog can be tricky. Dog food companies will use beef, chicken, bison, and salmon to add protein to their food, just to name a few. The type of protein that's recommended for your dog is up for debate as what it mainly comes down to is the actual amount of protein and other nutrients your dog needs. I started my dog on a beef and sweet potato diet when he got to adulthood. I went with a grain-free food and bought into the hype that grains are bad for dogs. I didn't notice any outward problems with him on this diet, but noticed he wasn't as excited about walks and was shedding a lot.

After a trip to the vet to make sure he wasn't physically ill, my vet made a recommendation that I still stick to, to this day. She recommended that I put my dog on a diet that consisted of salmon meal. Many of the top dog

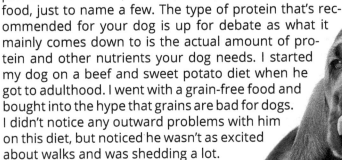

foods out there have an option that has fish as the main source of protein, whether it be salmon or whitefish. For my dog, the reason the vet recommended it was because the fatty acids found in salmon would be good for his coat and give it a noticeable sheen. After doing some research, I have chosen to keep him on a salmon diet because, first of all, it doesn't make him gassy. Second, I did see a huge reduction in his shedding after switching his foods. He still sheds a lot because he's a Bloodhound, but not nearly as much as he used to. And the last reason I chose to stick with a salmon-based protein source is because the omega 3 fatty acids are supposed to help with cognitive function and intelligence. Being a Bloodhound, he needs all the help in that department that he can get.

Different Types of Foods Available

As your pup grows, there are definitely food considerations you need to take into account to ensure they are getting what they need. Puppies shouldn't be eating adult dog food and vice versa. A lot of times, puppy food can be a bit softer, so as not to break your pup's teeth. But the main reason there are different foods for different life stages is because your dog will need different amounts of nutrients depending on their life cycle. You don't want to get an older dog all hopped up with excess protein when they don't need it or aren't able to expend the energy they get from it.

It is extremely important that you start your puppy off with a solid puppy food specifically designed for large dog breeds. Since Bloodhounds grow so much within their first year and develop a lot of muscle and skeletal mass, they require a food that provides the protein and calcium needed to support those structures. Also because of their growth spurts, they will eat a lot. It is not uncommon for Bloodhound puppies to go through 5-8 cups of dog food a day. As they get older, they will continue to be voracious eaters but you will need to temper their feeding schedule to ensure they don't become overweight.

Knowing when to switch between the different stages of food for your Bloodhound is something to discuss with your vet as it varies between dogs. It will depend on their activity level and size as you shouldn't switch away from puppy food until your hound is completely done growing. So as your pup grows, you will need to pay attention to them and their unique development to know exactly when to switch them onto different foods.

Keep in mind that moderation is the key with everything, and you don't want your pup putting on too much weight too fast, or they could have hip or skeletal problems later on. In all, pick a good puppy food that supports their growth and development, then switch them to an adult food with all the vitamins, fatty acids, and proteins they need when they stop growing, and as their energy levels decrease in old age, consider moving them to an elderly or senior dog food plan.

Raw Foods and Homemade Diets

There's a lot of talk nowadays about the benefits of feeding your dog a raw diet. This is definitely an option to consider, but depending on your situation, can become expensive really fast. A lot of people who choose to put their dogs on raw diets may be hunters or people with ample access to leftover animal scraps. The idea behind the raw diet is to restore your dog's more natural and primal diet and to get away from all the fillers and nonessential items found in commercial dog foods.

HELPFUL TIP
Feeding Tips for Preventing Bloat

Bloodhounds are one of the breeds prone to gastric torsion, better known as bloat. To reduce the odds of your Bloodhound developing bloat, feed him at least twice a day from bowls on the floor rather than in a raised feeder. Better yet, give him a slow-feeder bowl or treat puzzle toy to slow his eating down even further and reduce how much air he swallows while he gobbles his food.

Some debate exists about the digestibility of cooked foods when it comes to domesticated animals. Being that the cooking process dramatically changes the chemical structure of the food that is being cooked and creates complex carbohydrates in the process, some people argue that our dogs' bodies cannot process those things as efficiently. Raw food and meat provides the protein and other nutrients in an unaltered and natural state.

While there may be truth to the idea that certain processed foods can't be digested as easily by our dogs, their status as man's best friend has also helped change that. As humans and dogs have evolved together, dogs have been exposed to and fed a lot of the same foods their human counterparts have eaten. Since humans cook most of their food, many scientists believe that our dogs' gastrointestinal tract has adapted to be more tolerant of cooked foods. In other words, our dogs have lost a lot of their wild nature as we bred them to be closer to us as pets. So if you decide to put your dog on a diet of raw meats, make sure it's also supplemented with certain vegetables as we mentioned above. They really do need a wide array of nutrients that they cannot get from meat alone.

Human Food and Table Scraps

As you'll soon come to learn, Bloodhounds are hungry dogs. They eat almost constantly. And, since they are big dogs that can easily rest their heads on a dinner table, they will want to eat what you are eating as well. Try to limit the table scraps that you feed to your dog as feeding them will reinforce undesirable behaviors and could pose some health risks to your pup. As we discussed before, food is a huge motivator for Bloodhounds, so if you reward them for begging at the dinner table, they will continue to do it. You want to be able to have guests over for dinner without having a drooly Bloodhound resting their head in your guests' lap, so teach them that when humans eat, Bloodhounds go somewhere else. This is easier said than done, but you can employ the use of chew toys or treats to entertain the dog while you eat.

The other negative thing associated with feeding your dog table scraps is that there are a lot of items which simply don't mesh well with a dog's stomach. We all know that chocolate is bad for dogs, and there are many other items that dogs just can't digest. Things commonly used in cooking like onion and lemons, while not outright toxic to dogs, can cause stomach irritation and diarrhea. It's best to separate human food and dog food so that your pup stays healthy and learns not to bug while the humans are eating.

Weight Management

So now that you've learned some introductory lessons about what and when to feed your Bloodhound, it's time to tie it all together by explaining the why behind it. Above all else, the main thing to consider when choosing a food and the frequency of feedings is your dog's weight. Bloodhounds are enormous. But while they stand tall, they are lean and muscular dogs. Because of how much they eat, they have the propensity to gain too much weight, which can cause health problems. It's said that with a Bloodhound, you should be able to feel their ribcage and see a distinct indent where their body transitions from ribs to stomach. Now, of course you don't want to starve your dog, but you don't want them to be too fat and happy either. Bloodhounds are already prone to hip problems, and the excess weight caused by overeating can just increase that risk.

Try to maintain a good balance of diet and exercise with your pup to keep them in tip-top shape. Their weight, dietary needs, and exercise requirements will change throughout their life, so try to be invested and in tune with their outward appearance. If they start putting on too much weight, try to get them out more to exercise and burn some of the excess calories off. If they start putting on a bunch of weight and are out running around like crazy, maybe it's time to look at changing their food because their body may have started processing nutrients differently.

HELPFUL TIP
Is Your Bloodhound Obese?

Due to their stocky build, Bloodhounds are often overweight or obese because their owners think that's the way their dog is supposed to look. You should be able to feel your Bloodhound's ribs, and he should have a waistline when seen from above and the side.

In the long run, we all want our Bloodhounds to be cuddly and gentle giants, but we want them to get that way through proper training and exercise, not because they are too fat to move. So be invested in your dog's diet as they are relying on you to give them what they need to lead long and healthy lives.

CHAPTER 17
Grooming Your Bloodhound

"Bloodhounds are not a high maintenance grooming breed. I recommend bathing once a week and brushing them on a regular basis will help reduce shedding. Cleaning their eyes is one of the most important things to do. They tend to drain sometimes because some of them have deep pockets around their eyes."

Kim Dillon
Sandstone Kennels

A Bloodhound's Coat and Shedding

I'm pretty sure that we've established that owning a Bloodhound requires a strong stomach. They are notoriously dirty creatures and due to their unique physical appearance, have many folds and flaps of skin designed perfectly to catch dirt and grime and all sorts of other gross substances. When a Bloodhound drinks water, their ears will undoubtedly get wet in the process and will then drag along the ground, creating a muddy goo which dries into a crust when hardened. Their large lips and jowls are great places to store extra pieces of kibble and food for later, and when left for long periods of time, will mix with the saliva to create some sort of chunky concoction more suitable for a horror movie. Their wrinkles form perfect vessels for drool and moisture to collect and fester.

HELPFUL TIP
Reducing Shedding

Bloodhounds shed short, splinter-like hairs that can embed themselves into your clothing and furniture. To reduce how much hair your dog sheds around your home, brush your Bloodhound with a rubber curry brush a few times a week and run a Furminator or similar de-shedding tool over him no more than once a week.

All in all, Bloodhounds are a bit disgusting. They aren't really a great fit for someone who loves everything to be neat and odor free because Bloodhounds themselves aren't neat

FUN FACT

Slobber Slingers

Did you know that when a Bloodhound shakes, it can sling slobber as far as 20 feet? That means no surface in your home is safe from slobber.

or odor free. In fact, they are quite the opposite. They are a hot mess most of the time and they come with a very distinctive hound smell. It's hard to describe, but it's akin to a musty, yeasty smell. I saved this part to put at the end of the book because I didn't want to scare you away too soon. Now that you're in it and there's no turning back, let's try to focus on some tips that will keep your dog as clean and sanitary as possible.

Bloodhounds are technically a short-haired dog, but trust me, they have no shortage of hair. They do shed quite a bit and keeping that hair off your floors and out of your food can be difficult. Thigs like brushing, baths, and the right diet can help combat the problem, but won't ever completely alleviate it. I use a brush that has bristles on one side and then larger metal tines on the other. The bristles side will help smooth the hair and clean it a bit as it removes surface debris. The metal tines will actually penetrate the top coat and go down to their undercoat. This is where most of the shedding occurs and the tines will help dislodge any loose fur. Bloodhounds keep a pretty consistent coat on year round, and aren't like other breeds where they bulk up in the winter months. This is a good thing because they won't be losing giant tufts of hair all over the place when it starts warming up in spring. But at the same time, it just means they will shed consistently year round.

Photo Courtesy of Vicky Pittsley

Nail Trimming Techniques

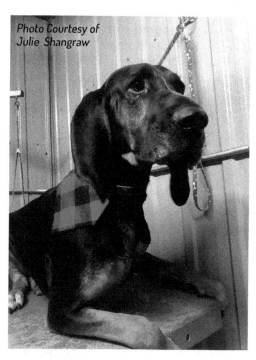

Photo Courtesy of
Julie Shangraw

Once you've come to terms with the fact that your Bloodhound's excess fur will be inescapable, the next task you have to overcome is trimming their nails. Trimming a dog's nails can feel a bit scary because if you cut them too short, your dog will start bleeding and it will be a traumatic experience for everyone. But cutting their nails is extremely important as you don't want them to break one off unintentionally.

With proper exercise and care, your dog should actually keep their nails at a reasonable length all on their own. When they are out on walks and running around, they will naturally wear their nails down without your aid. But that's the best-case scenario. Odds are you will have to trim their nails from time to time and with a Bloodhound, even a small task like this can seem insurmountable. First off, you have to keep them still. Second, you have to make sure they aren't afraid of the clippers. As we now know, Bloodhounds can be scared of the most random things, so nail clippers may prove to become a worthy adversary for them.

The best way to find out how to clip a dog's nails is to take them in and get it professionally done once or twice. Watch your vet and pay attention to just how short they take the nails down. Again, you don't want to cut too short, or your dog will bleed and you'll have blood everywhere. There are products out there that will help stop the bleeding if this does occur, but household products like baking soda can also be used to help clot the blood.

When you're ready to undertake the task of cutting your dog's nails, try introducing them to the clippers slowly. Have some treats available and let the dog get used to the idea of having the clippers around. If you try to hold them down and introduce the clippers, they will most likely freak out and make the task that much more difficult. You may want to give your dog a new toy or a treat of some sort that will keep them occupied so you can get close and keep them in control. Trim the nails down, clipping off a little at a time to make sure you don't go too short. The nail should be short enough that it doesn't hit the ground when they are walking. Essentially, you shouldn't be able to hear them clicking down the hallway to you. If you do go too short and accidentally clip your dog's quick as they call it, don't worry. It's not too painful and won't cause any long-term issues. Simply reinforce them with a treat to distract them from the pain and also distract them so they don't associate the clippers with pain.

If you have to take a break in between nails, then so be it. Take it slow and don't overwhelm your dog. Try to make it a pleasant and relaxing experience so you can continue to do it at home and not pay a professional to do it every time. Cutting your Bloodhound's nails can be easy if you introduce it right. So just focus on making it an enjoyable and reward-filled experience for them. It's much easier if they are trained to enjoy it rather than fighting it, because wrangling a nervous Bloodhound is near impossible.

Cleaning Ears, Folds, and Flaps

"Bloodhounds are known for their long floppy ears, and wrinkles. I recommend keeping their ears clean by wiping them with a warm rag weekly. It is also a good idea to inspect wrinkly areas daily to ensure they are dry."

Heather Pearson
Black Diamond Bloodhounds & Bracco Italianos

Brushing your dog and trimming their nails are basic grooming requirements for pretty much any dog, but your Bloodhound has some unique challenges you will have to deal with as well. All their wrinkles, folds, and flaps are what give them their iconic appearance, but also can be a sore spot when it comes to their comfort. All that excess skin is great at capturing moisture, excess food, and dirt, so keeping them clean is essential in making sure your pup stays comfortable and itch free.

Photo Courtesy of
Ashley and Spencer Hall

Dermatitis is a real concern for Bloodhounds because all that dirt and moisture can cause the skin to rub together and become itchy. Many Bloodhound owners talk about their dogs itching almost constantly, and it is usually caused by inflammation or dry skin caused by irritation from rubbing. This is something that is kind of hard to avoid as you can't follow your dog around with a towel drying off every inch of them all day every day. But just be mindful of it when giving them a bath or if they come into the house after running around. Get a damp towel and rub them all over, getting into their folds and flaps, and especially their ears. You want to get as much dirt and debris out of there as possible.

After cleaning those areas, do it again with a dry towel and dry them off as much as possible. What you're trying to combat is chafing and a buildup of moisture. Bloodhounds' ears are especially prone to infection due to their large size. The ear flaps cover up their ear canals, creating a perfect breeding ground for bacteria that love dark, damp places. You don't want to stick your finger all the way into their ear canal, but you want to gently rub off any excess grime or ear wax that you find in there. After baths, it's good to run your fingers along the inside of their mouths to get out any old and crusty food as well.

What I'm trying to get at here is that you want to make sure you clean those dark and not often seen places. If there's a spot you can't normally pet on your dog because his excess skin hides it, get in there with a towel and dry it out from time to time. Don't be afraid to give them a bath either. A little bit of peanut butter on the wall can make this an easy task as they will be focused on eating up their delicious treat while you get to work cleaning all the nooks and crannies. Just be aware that after you expose them to all that moisture, you have to dry them off thoroughly. Get familiar with all of their hard to reach places. They can't reach them by themselves and will be a happier and itch-free dog if you give them the care they need.

Keeping the Nose in Tip-Top Condition – Nose Butter and Other Items

Dry skin is a big problem for Bloodhounds. They are prone to getting it in their folds and flaps, but can also get it on their noses too. Because their noses are so often down to the ground smelling things, they have the propensity to get a lot of dirt on them which can dry out their nose. I jokingly tell my wife that my dog's nose is the only useful part on him, so it's important to keep it in tip-top shape. There are products that exist that will help you moisturize your pup's nose if it does in fact become dry and cracked. I bought some nose butter for my boy and apply it every so often when I can tell he's been digging in the dirt. As with everything, the key is moderation as keeping his nose moisturized is something that he should do all on his own, but it doesn't hurt to spoil your pup every now and then. There are other creams and butters out there for the pads on their paws or for the calluses that will form on their elbows and knees. While these items aren't necessary and are oftentimes rejected by purists for making your Bloodhound too sensitive, they are aids that you can use to make your dog more comfortable and soft. Bloodhounds are a very tough breed and work hard, so in my opinion, it's okay to spoil them sometimes with a spa treatment.

CHAPTER 18
Basic Health Care

Visiting the Vet

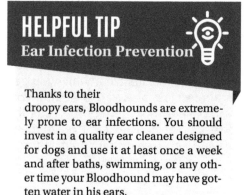

HELPFUL TIP
Ear Infection Prevention

Thanks to their droopy ears, Bloodhounds are extremely prone to ear infections. You should invest in a quality ear cleaner designed for dogs and use it at least once a week and after baths, swimming, or any other time your Bloodhound may have gotten water in his ears.

As a pet owner, it's imperative that you find yourself a good vet who knows the ins and outs of your specific breed. They are the ones you will rely on to keep your dog healthy and will guide you into how to prolong your dog's life into a full and happy one. Follow their lead and keep their numbers on speed dial. Bloodhounds are prone to certain ailments that may leave you needing a vet in an emergency. They will be the ones to let you know everything from when to vaccinate to how to care for your dog in old age. They will guide you on what food to feed and how to keep your dog happy. Essentially, your vet will be your guru in all things that can't be googled.

When your dog is younger, there are some more basic healthcare items which you will have to do as general maintenance. These are things that all dogs require, but there will be certain nuances with your Bloodhound when it comes to things like neutering and spaying. The nuances are the reason why you want a vet who knows your breed extensively. Having a knowledgeable advocate for my hound made making decisions about his healthcare that much easier. As with many things Bloodhound related, there are a million different opinions on when and how to do certain things. The following are what I've learned through my experiences so use them as a starting point, but consult your vet and do your own research before making any decisions that could impact the health of your dog.

Vaccinations

One of the first things you will have to do with your dog health wise is get them vaccinated. Most puppies will come with their first set of shots when you purchase or rescue them. These all-in-one shots actually fight against a variety of ailments including distemper and other illnesses. Some people will choose to administer these shots at home and many vets will sell you the shots to do yourself. It's really not a hard thing to do, especially when they are puppies, but if you don't feel comfortable administering the shots yourself, take them to your vet or a shot clinic.

I've found that getting my dog to the vet is the biggest part of the battle. Once we are there, he barely feels the vaccinations as they usually go in the scruff of his neck where he has a lot of excess skin. Of course, this comes with its own complications as making sure the vaccine gets to the spot it's intended for can be a bit tricky. But overall, the shots don't really seem to faze my pup and our visits have been relatively drama free.

After the all-in-one shots, you are going to need to get your dog treated for rabies. This is usually state mandated and all dogs are required to have their rabies shot. Once vaccinated against rabies, your dog will get a special tag to put on their collar to indicate they are up to date on their shots. Your dog will usually receive their first rabies shot within their first year of life, and will then get a follow-up the next year as a booster. After that, it depends on the state to determine how often the vaccine needs to be renewed. Check with your vet to see how often you need to update your Bloodhound to make sure they are healthy and not at risk for a rabies infection. As a pet owner, it's your duty to make sure your pet is vaccinated. It protects your dog and it helps protect other dogs they come in contact with as well. Stay consistent with their shots and make sure to build a good relationship with your vet to ensure your dog is healthy and doesn't have any lapses in their vaccinations.

Heartworm Prevention

The next step in preventative care for your dog is heartworm prevention. Heartworm is an ailment that can affect any dog, at any time, in any part of the world. Many people feel that if they don't live in warm and wet climates, they don't have to worry about heartworm. This is because heartworm is carried by mosquitos. The mosquito bites the dog and infects them. The larva that comes from that bite then attacks the dog's circulatory system, lodging itself in their heart and lungs. As the larva start to reproduce, they clog up arteries and can indeed be life threatening if

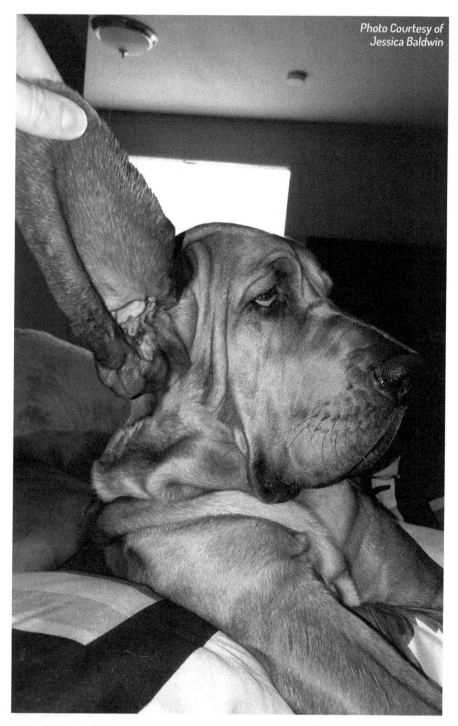

Photo Courtesy of Jessica Baldwin

left untreated. Prevention for heartworm can be a bit costly, but many vets will offer subscription-like services where you can get discounts if you stay on top of it and return for a visit every six months.

Heartworm medication comes in many different forms from pills to topical treatments to shots. Usually the pills and injections last longer and provide better care as a lot of the topical can rub off or fail to make skin contact and be absorbed into your dog's system. While some people think that they don't need to worry about heartworm because they don't live near water and mosquitos aren't a big worry, I would say that while the risk may be minimized, it's never fully eradicated. Preventing heartworm is a relatively easy step to take to be extra sure that your dog doesn't fall victim to its deadly effects. After all, you put such an investment into buying, training, and loving your Bloodhound, it doesn't hurt to take extra precautions to make sure they are around for a long time.

Fleas and Ticks

Keep in mind that you aren't the only thing that's going to love your Bloodhound. Fleas and ticks will do anything they can to find a good host, and your Bloodhound's wrinkles are going to provide an excellent habitat for those parasites to exploit. Seeing as how your Bloodhound is going to spend a lot of time outside sniffing around, they will undoubtedly be sticking their noses in some less than desirable places. Those places are havens for fleas and ticks so it's your job to make sure they are protected against them.

Flea treatments are relatively easy to apply and will keep your dog from scratching or itching constantly. Most flea treatments are topical gels or liquids that you squeeze onto their back or neck. These topical ointments will protect your dog for a few weeks before needing to be reapplied. There are also wearable treatments that your dog can wear. When I take my Bloodhound camping, I do a liquid flea treatment and also put a preventative collar on him as well. Since I know he will be getting himself into a whole bunch of places with all the new smells, I try to double up on the prevention methods. It doesn't hurt to get a special flea shampoo to wash your dog with after long excursions in the outdoors either.

A lot of these ointments and wearable treatments will also help deter ticks from latching on. Your Bloodhound's folds and flaps provide a great place for ticks to latch on and hitch a ride on your dog. Ticks are little black parasites that can infect your dog with multiple different diseases like Lyme disease and can even cause something called tick paralysis. Preventing this is relatively easy if you pay attention to your dog and all their folds and flaps like we talked about in the grooming section above. Make sure to regularly check all the crevices on your dog for ticks, and, if you find one, remove it completely. Rubbing alcohol will do a good job of killing the tick, but you also have to remove it from your dog's body to prevent further infection. Use a pair of tweezers to pull the tick off of your dog after soaking the area with rubbing alcohol and make sure you get all of its pieces and parts off. Sometimes when pulling a tick off of your dog, its head will get stuck as it's the part that is attaching itself to them, so make sure all parts of the tick are removed. Also, make sure that you wear gloves when doing this as coming in contact with the blood inside of a tick is harmful to humans as well.

It may seem like our Bloodhounds are so big that something so small like a tick or flea could never bring them down, but the reality is they can. So be diligent in checking your dog for ticks after their adventures out into the world and take preventative measures by using topical ointments and collars to prevent them from ever hitching a ride on your dog in the first place.

Other Dogs and Canine Illnesses

One of the most important reasons to vaccinate and treat your dog for different ailments is not necessarily because of what they will randomly catch in nature, but because of what they could catch from other dogs. Fleas can jump between dogs and a trip to the dog park can leave you taking home some unwanted hitchhikers. It's important to remember that not all pet owners are as diligent and focused on their dog's health as you are. Many of the preventative measure you take will be simply to protect your dog from illnesses they may catch from interacting with other dogs.

One of the most common of these canine-borne illnesses is kennel cough. Kennel cough is actually a bronchitis caused by a bacteria called Bordetella. Bordetella infects your dog causing a respiratory illness and is highly contagious between animals. It gets the name kennel cough from the fact that dogs in kennels are often in close proximity so the bacteria has an opportunity to infect other dogs. But just because it's called kennel cough doesn't mean that it can only be caught in a kennel. If an infected dog comes in contact with yours at a dog park or out on a walk, it's possible for your dog to catch it.

Prevention and vaccination from Bordetella is relatively inexpensive and will save you from having a sick dog in your home. My vet joked that giving a Bloodhound a Bordetella vaccine is one of the easiest things to do because their nose is so big. The vaccine gets injected into their nose, so your Bloodhound's large nostrils are an excellent receptacle for it. If your dog is a social dog and enjoys puppy play dates frequently, it's recommended that you vaccinate against kennel cough annually every year. The vaccine is yet another simple and cheap way to ensure you aren't making any late-night emergency visits to the vet due to something that could easily be prevented.

Holistic Alternatives and Supplements

With all these different diseases and ailments, it may seem like keeping your dog healthy is a huge undertaking. But in reality, regular appointments with your veterinarian will help keep your dog in good shape. During the rest of the time while you aren't at the vet, you can also employ the help of holistic medicines to aid in their health. These alternatives should never be used as a cure-all or replacement for proper vaccines, but as supplements to help your dog.

With the emergence of CBD treatments, there are a variety of supplements that can be purchased for many different things. There are products found at your local pet store that will help encourage calmness or reduce anxiety in your dog. Many of these are loaded with tryptophan or melatonin and naturally reduce some of the energy in your dog. Be careful with these as they shouldn't be used as a way to tame your Bloodhound. As we discussed before, your Bloodhound's behavior is most likely a product of their environment and training, so simply sedating them isn't addressing the root problem.

But beyond stress relievers and calming aids, supplements exist to help give your dog's coat a nice sheen or help their joints. I've used treats in the past that have a variety of natural ingredients including mushrooms and herbs that aim to target a dog's joints and provide relief for them. A lot of these aids are extremely expensive and, like human holistic supplements, aren't always guaranteed to do what they say they do. But if you find your dog has a certain problem, you can always apply the use of supplements and pay attention to them to see if they have a desirable effect. Just use caution and make sure you are not medicating a dog for an undesirable behavior because that behavior is inconvenient, but rather that you are medicating to help the dog feel happier and healthier.

Pet Insurance

When all is said and done, you will most likely spend a lot of money on keeping your dog healthy, but emergencies happen outside of our control. We will talk about some of the Bloodhound-specific conditions next, but just know that unexpected trips to the vet can put you in a really tough spot when it comes to deciding what you are capable of treating for your best friend. Emergency vet visits can be costly and the last position you want to be in is not being able to provide care to save your dog's life due to budget concerns. Our dogs give their all to love us and be loyal to us, so it's our responsibility to care for them in their times of need.

Pet insurance can help alleviate some of the worry if you are placed in one of those tough scenarios. Pet insurance is like any other insurance you have where you pay monthly or yearly for it, but the costs are usually small compared to what you'll save when your dog needs an emergency operation or care. Shop around for pet insurance like you would car insurance. Make sure that you are armed with information and knowledge of what the most common emergencies you might encounter will be.

There are a lot of stories out there of people who pay for pet insurance only for it not to cover whatever it is their dog comes down with. Make sure you call the company if you go down this route and ask questions relating to Bloodhounds specifically. If your hound comes down with bloat, for example, the surgery to attempt to fix it can cost thousands of dollars. Try to ensure your insurance company will cover those surgeries so that you are not left having to wager your dog's life against your pocketbook. Pet insurance won't eliminate costs or prevent bad things from happening. But it can give you peace of mind in knowing that when the worst does happen, you are prepared to do everything you can for your best friend.

CHAPTER 19
Bloodhound-Specific Health

"Being a large dog, you have to watch for hip dysplasia and other bone/joint issues. Ask the breeder if there are any known issues in the lines or if the parents had any OFA testing done. Skin/major allergy issues can be another concern. Chronic ear infections, UTI's and eye inflammations are other issues that may be faced when owning a Bloodhound. Keeping eyes and ears clean will help deter those infections and giving your Bloodhound some yogurt each day will help fight urinary tract infections."

Nancy Boerner
Boerner's Bloodhounds

Common Health Problems

A lot of aspects of Bloodhound healthcare are general practices that every dog needs. But owning a Bloodhound comes with its own set of unique concerns that are especially prevalent in this breed. Things like bloat, hip dysplasia, and ectropion are all afflictions common to Bloodhounds, and while they may not necessarily be preventable, they are important to at least be aware of so you can know the warning signs. Some of these ailments appear later in life while others are a constant risk. Knowing about them will help you understand the breed a little bit and aid you in developing behaviors that can help minimize the risk that they occur.

Don't let this chapter scare you out of owning a Bloodhound. The risk is absolutely worth the reward. Just know that at some point during your hound's life, you will most likely encounter one of these ailments, so spend time preparing for them and knowing what to do when and if they occur. After all, Bloodhounds don't have the longest lifespan, so it's our duty to provide them with the happiest life they can possibly have in their short time with us.

Spaying and Neutering

Although this next topic isn't necessarily a disease or affliction, it's something you will have to consider early on in your dog's life. Spaying and neutering is a decision you will have to make depending on what you want to come out of your dog's life. If they are meant to be bred and carry on a bloodline, then this won't apply to you. But if your hound is going to be a house pet, odds are you will want to have them fixed. Neutering male dogs will help a lot with male aggression and their urge to mark territory. A buildup of testosterone can cause them to hold on to more of their wild roots and challenge you as the pack leader. With females, having an unexpected litter of puppies can be costly and inconvenient based on your household constraints.

HELPFUL TIP
Bloodhound Health Problems

Like all dog breeds, Bloodhounds are more prone to some health problems than others. Some of the more common health issues your Bloodhound might experience include:
- Hip or elbow dysplasia (joint problems)
- Skin fold dermatitis (wrinkle infections)
- Entropion or ectropion (eyelid problems)
- Bloat
- Epilepsy
- Hypothyroidism

But fixing your Bloodhound isn't as cut and dried as taking them to the vet and getting them snipped. Since Bloodhounds grow so much and are such large dogs, they require a strong skeletal structure to support that weight. Fixing your dog too young can cause certain hormones to decrease, ultimately stunting their development. It's usually best to wait until your Bloodhound is a year to eighteen months old to even begin considering getting them fixed. This will give their chest plate time to grow in and provide their bones ample opportunity to develop into a structure that can support their weight. During the sterilization procedure, vets can also surgically tack your dog's stomach, which will help prevent it from flipping and causing bloat. Sterilization is not only useful in curbing some of the exuberant Bloodhound behaviors your dog may exhibit, but can also be instrumental in preventing health problems later on. So talk to your vet, and develop a plan so that you can get your dog fixed at the right time to promote a long life for them.

Photo Courtesy of
Rebecca Byrd

Bloat

I've talked a little about bloat throughout this book, and really, it is deserving of its own chapter. Bloat is probably the scariest and most common emergency-related illness Bloodhounds are susceptible to. The scary part is that bloat can strike at almost any stage of life. Many young dogs have become affected by bloat and without immediate care, have perished in the process. The worst thing about bloat is that it is caused by something your dog needs to survive, which is eating. Bloat is a gastrointestinal affliction that is caused when air gets in your dog's stomach, causing it to flip or twist. When it twists, it cuts off your dog's blood supply, dropping their blood pressure and many times ending their life.

We established that Bloodhounds eat a lot, and because of what voracious eaters they are, they can oftentimes gobble up their food so fast that they get air down in their stomach, causing bloat. Exercising right after eating can also cause their stomachs to flip. It's because of this that many owners will get food bowls that are raised, which help slow the dog's eating and discourages them from gulping down so much excess air while they gobble up their food. There are also mats or feeding trays designed to spread the food out so that your dog is eating one bit of food at a time, rather than inhaling mouthfuls.

Since your dog has to eat to survive, special considerations must be taken after your dog eats to prevent bloat. Make sure that your dog doesn't run around or get too wild after eating so they don't cause their stomach to flip. This can be done through training, but many times, Bloodhounds are simply too energetic to contain and don't understand what could happen if they jump around too much. I've read where people will put their dog in their crate or separate them from other animals for up to an hour after they eat to allow the food to digest.

While this is a good preventative measure, it may not always be realistic due to how much Bloodhounds eat. The best way to prevent it is to slow the rate at which your dog ingests food and encourage calm behavior afterward. Teach other household members about the danger of bloat so they don't rile the dog up after they eat. If, in the terrible circumstance your dog becomes affected with bloat or you even suspect it, call your vet right away. Symptoms include lethargy and excessive drooling. The drooling part can be hard to determine since these animals salivate so much to begin with, but you will notice they are sick because their saliva will be more liquid like, clear and more excessive than normal. Again, this is not something to be taken lightly, and if you even suspect your dog has come down with bloat, call your vet immediately. It could end up saving your pup's life.

Happy Tail

Another ailment Bloodhounds are prone to has a weird name that may seem somewhat deceiving. Happy tail is an injury dogs incur on their tails from hitting it on things, causing it to rupture and bleed. This often occurs when your hound gets excited and starts wagging their tail. Because of their size, even their tail wagging is exuberant and has so much force that it can actually cause the skin to split. The result is a bleeding tail which then, when wagged, spurts blood on walls and the floor. If left untreated, it can cause the tail to get infected and result in amputation. The best way to prevent it is to try and greet your dog in an open area away from hard surfaces. Try to eliminate the possibility of them wagging their tail into something that can hurt it. It's obviously easier said than done, but make a concerted effort to get them away from things they can whack their tail on. Unfortunately, if it continues to happen, the only real way to stop it is amputation and your dog's appearance will be a little less iconic without their tail standing straight up when following a scent. This is just another example of Bloodhounds not knowing their own strength and accidentally hurting themselves in the process.

Ear and Yeast Infections

As we mentioned in the grooming section, your Bloodhound will run the risk of ear and yeast infections from a buildup of moisture. As much as we try to dry our dogs off and keep their folds and flaps clean, it's inevitable that some moisture will find its way in and cause problems. A Bloodhound's ears are especially susceptible to infections and beyond some basic wiping and cleaning, not much can be done to prevent them. It's good to talk to your vet about this beforehand and get on a regular regimen of cleaning your dog's ears out.

Odds are you will smell a problem exists before seeing it. Your dog will display signs of scratching at or shaking their heads to try to relieve some of the pain in their ears. For my hound, I can always tell when his ears need some care because of two things. First, his ears will take on a distinctly yeasty smell. It's an undeniable odor and can be so strong it will make your eyes water. The other way I can tell is that when he barks, his will start shaking his head back and forth afterward. It's almost as if when he barks there's a ringing in his head and he can't get it to stop. Whenever either of those things happens, I know it's time to treat his ears.

You can get prescribed medication and ear wash from your vet which work wonders and will clear it up in a few days, but you can also use

Photo Courtesy of
Brenda Crain

some home remedies as well. Mixing some warm water and apple cider vinegar together works pretty well as a home remedy. You want to put some of the wash into their ear, just a few drops at a time, and then massage it in. Bloodhounds have some large lumps and glands on the rear of their ears, so give your dog a nice massage and make sure the medicine works its way down into their ear canal. Repeat this treatment every day until the problem clears up. Nothing you do will really be able to prevent an infection from happening, but knowing how to identify when it starts bothering your dog will help you treat it before it gets out of control.

Hip Dysplasia

As your pup gets older, their weight, size, and years of running around will undoubtedly start to cause problems for them. Their hips and joints support so much weight throughout their lives that it's only natural for their joints to eventually give out. Hip dysplasia is common in Bloodhounds because of their size. It's just part of the breed. Think of dysplasia as a form of arthritis and how it affects humans. It affects your Bloodhound in similar ways. It will make it hard for them to do things they used to do like jump and run and play.

As your dog gets older, you want to help minimize the stress they are putting on their back legs by making your home easier for them to navigate. This may mean putting steps next to your bed if they are used to sleeping with you or stopping them from hopping up on the couch. You may have to start lifting them up when they get into your car so they aren't trying to lift all their weight on their own.

Hip dysplasia can't be cured or eliminated, but it can be treated to make your dog more comfortable. Veterinarians can prescribe joint medications or anti-inflammatory drugs to alleviate some of the pain caused by the joint degradation. Again, holistic treatments like CBD oils are said to help with joint inflammation and can be used to make your dog more comfortable and supplement any other techniques used to alleviate their joint pain.

Eventually though, after years of carrying their big goofy bodies around, their hips will begin to fail them. One of the hardest things to witness is seeing your hound, once filled with boundless energy and enthusiasm, start to falter as they reach their sunset. Again, you can't stop it from happening, so prepare for it and make sure you are ready to keep your dog comfortable and as pain free as possible.

Cancer

I wanted to spend the majority of this book talking about how happy and goofy Bloodhounds are, rather than weighing it down with some of the sad realities of owning them. Beyond what we talked about above, it is said that one-third of dogs will receive a cancer diagnosis in their lives. Bloodhounds also have a condition called ectropion where their eyelids can roll in or outward due to the weight of their skin pulling down on their face over the years. I wish that there were more things that could be done to prevent the stuff we talked about in this chapter. But the reality is, it comes with the breed. Just like their drool and their baying, their health problems are just part of the territory.

Preventative Measures

This may sound cheesy, but loving them is really the best preventative measure you can take. They are frustrating as all get out at times, but they will also bring so much joy into your life that you will wonder how you lived without them. By giving your Bloodhound love and enjoying them every second, you are fulfilling their sole obligation in this world. As their owner, your job is to take care of them and keep them alive, but their job is to be loyal to you. Take the time to prepare for the eventuality of your dog experiencing some of the ailments listed above. Your preparation and readiness will prove invaluable in your dog's biggest time of need.

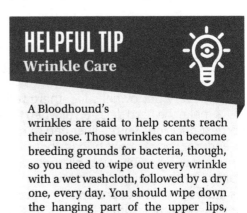

HELPFUL TIP
Wrinkle Care

A Bloodhound's wrinkles are said to help scents reach their nose. Those wrinkles can become breeding grounds for bacteria, though, so you need to wipe out every wrinkle with a wet washcloth, followed by a dry one, every day. You should wipe down the hanging part of the upper lips, called the flews, after every meal.

CHAPTER 20

Long and Full Lives – How to Love and How to Say Goodbye

Life Expectancy of Bloodhounds

In every pet owner's life, there will come a time when you have to make the hard decision of when to let your pet go. It will be one of the hardest decisions you've ever had to make and will be almost unbearable to endure. Losing a pet brings about a grief similar to that when we lose a human companion. After all, these animals have been our best friends, waiting for us when we get home, and living to please us their whole lives. It's natural to want to prolong their lives and keep them with us as long as possible, but more often than not, the compassionate thing to do is to let them go. There are decisions you will have to make about how you want to go about this when your Bloodhound's time comes. It is a deeply personal experience and can easily be overshadowed by its sadness.

But I'm going to try to position it another way. Don't imagine it as letting your dog go, but rather as yet another training exercise. Only this time, after spending years training your dog how to behave, what not to chew on and to pee anywhere except your floors, it's time for you yourself to be trained in something new. Use this as an opportunity to be strong for your dog, to show them utmost compassion, and, no matter how hard it may seem, to be by their side to the end.

I remember being a kid and taking my golden retriever to the vet to put her down. I was nine years old and couldn't bear the idea of watching her die. So I ran away as far and fast as I could, thinking in my little head that if I didn't see it happen then it wasn't real. To this day, I regret that decision. My dog had spent her life protecting me and loving me, and in her most vulnerable moment I wasn't there to show her she had seen her job to completion. Saying goodbye is a learning experience and it is our obligation as pet owners to make sure your dog's sunset is as beautiful and comfortable as possible.

Of course, we want our dogs to live as long as possible. With Bloodhounds, as long as possible may still seem like it's not enough. Due to their size and propensity for health issues, the average life expectancy of a Bloodhound is 8-10 years. It's almost as if they are so energetic and exuberant early on that they just run out of gas in their later years. The majority of Bloodhounds reach the end of their lives due to illness, but if you are one of the lucky few who gets to keep your hound into old age, then cherish that time. Too many of us lose our Bloodhounds earlier than we were expecting, and would trade anything for just one more day with them.

When you pair this life expectancy with their propensity for life-threatening and sudden-onset illnesses, you will begin to see why it's been so important to be patient with your dog through the years. At the time, their digging and drooling and baying and all the other Bloodhound behaviors we talked about seem frustrating and make you second-guess why you ever got a Bloodhound in the first place. But when they're gone, you'll miss those things and wonder how life can go on without them. You've spent years figuring out a routine and changing your life to fit a Bloodhound into it, and when they're gone, life will seem a little less bright.

To me, other dogs just don't add up anymore. Sure, they're calmer and cleaner and easier to handle, but they also seem a bit boring. I found myself missing the chaos and still walking around with a mop looking for slobber bombs on the wall. No matter when it happens, it always seems like it's too soon. With that being said, I won't judge anyone if they ever found themselves muttering life-threatening threats under their breath from time to time during their Bloodhound's life. They probably tried your patience, frustrated you to no end, and got more dirty looks than you can count, but they almost certainly left an indelible mark on any life they were so lucky to have come across.

Basics of Senior Dog Care

If you do get to see your dog into their senior years, there are some aspects of senior canine healthcare to be aware of. For the most part, you just want to remain diligent and focused on how your dog behaves. You've been with them for so long at this point that you will know when they aren't feeling well or are acting differently. They can't tell us when they are in pain, so pay attention to if their routine is changing. They may not get up as quickly when you get home or they may not wanna go outside and lie in the sun as much. They may know their time is running out and want to be by your side as much as possible. Just pay attention to them, and if their behavior changes or you notice them having trouble getting around, don't put off taking them to the vet to get checked out.

I know I put off taking my older dog to the vet because I was so afraid they'd tell me it was time to say goodbye. But I was being selfish, and wasn't acknowledging the struggle and pain my dog was most likely enduring. Taking them into the vet can help you identify what you can do to make their walk to their sunset more comfortable. Your vet can identify joint issues and recommend treatments or they can provide advice on any foods that may provide your dog with the right stuff to keep them happy. Whatever it is, a relationship with your vet is just as important in the late stages of life as it is when they are a puppy. Talking to them will also help you begin to prepare a plan for what happens when one of the hardest days of your life arrives and you have say goodbye.

Photo Courtesy of
Nancy Boerner
Boerner's Bloodhounds

Signs of Failing Health

Since you've been by your dog's side for their whole lives, you will notice when things are different with them. You may notice that the light in their eyes starts to fade or that they are just slower when they are getting around. Some people say dogs will tell you when they are ready. There's something about the way they look at you, almost as if they are trying to connect with your soul so they aren't ever forgotten. They may even revert to puppy behav-

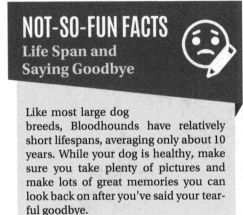

NOT-SO-FUN FACTS
Life Span and
Saying Goodbye

Like most large dog breeds, Bloodhounds have relatively short lifespans, averaging only about 10 years. While your dog is healthy, make sure you take plenty of pictures and make lots of great memories you can look back on after you've said your tearful goodbye.

iors and start having accidents on the floor. Try not to get too mad at them, they are trying their hardest to be a good dog. But as time goes on, some things are outside of their control. Sometimes it's obvious that something is wrong. Many times, a dog's hips will just give out, you'll notice them unable to get up, or you'll have to help them move around or get outside.

But many times, it's not as clear. Your dog will seemingly fight through anything to spend just another good day with you. That's why as an owner, you have to pay attention to them and always ask yourself about their quality of life. If they still have life in their eyes and bursts of puppy-like energy, then perhaps they're just starting to wear down and their time isn't here yet. But if you find yourself providing them hospice-like care, it's time to let go. Both you and your dog will try to hold on because you don't want to cheat each other out of some more time together. But being able to identify that they just aren't who they used to be and are struggling to do normal things will help you make the decision of when it's time to let them go. Don't prolong life for selfish reasons; be compassionate and make sure your dog is happy and comfortable through the end.

Being Compassionate and Being by Their Side Until the End

Photo Courtesy of
Tracy Harrison
Sage Mountain Bloodhounds

When the time comes, don't make my mistake. Be with them when it happens. If you take them into your vet's office or call a vet out to your home, stay by their side. Pet them as they close their eyes and go to sleep, whispering in their ear that they were the best dog you ever had. Your voice was their guiding light for all those years; let them hear it as they take their final journey. The last thing you want is for them to be surrounded by people they don't know in a scary environment. They're already going to be scared because they just don't feel like they're supposed to, so be their Alpha. Now more than ever, they need you to be strong and confident as they face the fading light of their sunset. Surround them with love and family. They need to see that they did their job and can leave knowing they worked hard and protected your family to the best of their ability.

After they're gone, treat them with dignity. It's not uncommon for people to cremate their best friends and put them to rest at home where they spent their lives. Not everyone will have the luxury of being able to bury their dog at home, so I strongly recommend looking into cremation services for them. If you live in a city, the process of disposing of your pet can seem extremely insensitive and impersonal. Most funeral homes will offer pet cremation services, and this will allow you to keep your pet around or spread their ashes in a place where they can enjoy a sunny day for the rest of time. As you did up until the end, treat them with compassion after they're gone too. Having a place to go to remind you of all the smiles and tears and slobber you went through over the past years will be invaluable in honoring their memory.

When your dog's time comes, know you are not alone in the pain and grief you feel. We have all had pets in our lives, but yours was the best. They were the most special animal that ever graced your life. You did one of the hardest things you could do by choosing to raise a Bloodhound. The only thing harder than raising and training them is saying goodbye and watching them go into their sunset.

I hope that you learned something while reading this book. I am confident you'll do your best to train your Bloodhound and love them into being the best dog you ever had. Wear your drool-stained clothes as a badge of courage and as a testament that you tamed this wild beast. We are Bloodhound owners, now and forever. Give your Bloodhound an extra kiss on the sniffer for me tonight. I promise you won't break it.

Printed in the USA
CPSIA information can be obtained
at www.ICGtesting.com
LVHW020043181223
766711LV00005B/80